"Kids come to school wide-eyed and ready for a great experience. Our job is to cultivate that opportunity and create a place that kids want to run to every morning. *Hacking Early Learning* gets to both the heart and mind of our youngest learners. The practical strategies allow the reader to set up an environment that works for everyone in the learning community. If you work with kids, or adults who work with kids, *Hacking Early Learning* is an essential component to your leadership toolbox."

JOE SANFELIPPO
SUPERINTENDENT, FALL CREEK SCHOOLS,
CO-AUTHOR OF *HACKING LEADERSHIP*

"*Hacking Early Learning* is the book every early learning leader should read. As teachers and administrators become increasingly pressed to do it all, there is less and less time to do anything, making true reform difficult. In response to this, Jessica Cabeen has put together a guide for improving early learning environments that focuses on the policies and practices that will yield the most bang for the buck, providing strategies that even the busiest of us can put into practice. The stories sprinkled throughout make the book a truly engaging read and one that will no doubt influence the field positively for many years to come."

ADAM HOLLAND
DIRECTOR, NORTH CAROLINA EARLY LEARNING NETWORK,
FRANK PORTER GRAHAM CHILD DEVELOPMENT INSTITUTE

"As I pored through the pages of *Hacking Early Learning* by Jessica Cabeen, I was reminded once again that the best educators see themselves as learners first. Research tells us the early years of learning are vital for all kids. However, Jessica gives us a practitioner's perspective with specific examples and steps to guide and lead us in supporting their path to success. This book reminded me of how much I don't know about the early years and will serve as a tremendous resource for me and for all who read it."

JIMMY CASAS
EDUCATOR, LEADERSHIP COACH, AUTHOR, SPEAKER

"Jessica Cabeen is not afraid to say she's learned from her mistakes and misconceptions. But it is those mistakes and misconceptions that qualify her to write this book, with its wonderfully user-friendly format. For each problem specified, there is a hack and actionable advice presented as "What You Can Do Tomorrow" and "A Blueprint for Full Implementation." Jessica's leadership is informed by both head and heart and, because of that, her wisdom will be of value to those who wish to teach and lead in the early childhood field."

RAE PICA
EARLY CHILDHOOD EDUCATION KEYNOTE SPEAKER AND CONSULTANT
AUTHOR OF *WHAT IF EVERYBODY UNDERSTOOD CHILD DEVELOPMENT?*

"*Hacking Early Learning* is an outstanding book written by an outstanding school leader. It is not often that I get excited about a book simply by reading the Table of Contents, but that is what happened with this book. Each subsequent powerful chapter of this important book contains keen insights based on research and years of authentic experience. Cabeen shares practical ideas for making the early learning years for our nation's youth exactly what they should be and must be, experiences marked by play and exploration, but also laser-focused on learning for all. This book is a must-read—not only for early learning educators, but for educators at all levels!"

DR. JEFFREY ZOUL
LEADERSHIP COACH, AUTHOR, SPEAKER

"*Hacking Early Learning* brings together a wonderful blend of big ideas, practical solutions, and motivation for the reader. This is perfect for a wide range of leaders and educators at all levels because of the specific tips and insights that Jessica has provided from her own experiences and those that she has gathered from other experts around the country. She challenges you to be better for students, families, and colleagues in a way that is highly motivational and leaves you with a feeling of, "Yes, I can do this!" Jessica's amazing successes as a school leader give credibility and weight to her shared knowledge so that the readers feel empowered and confident in turn-keying these strategies into a plan of action to be successful at their schools. You're going to love reading this book and want to share it with others!"

ANDY JACKS
AWARD-WINNING PRINCIPAL AND CO-FOUNDER OF *#DADSASPRINCIPALS*

"Jessica has written an extremely practical guide for ALL educators who work with or influence students in the Pre-K to third-grade realms. Her voice as a seasoned Early Childhood Educator and passion for fostering developmentally appropriate learning in high-quality settings is woven throughout every page. Jessica presents practical ideas for leaders that can be implemented immediately, such as shadowing an early-year student for a day, while also defining "blueprints" explaining long-range approaches to address the problem presented in each chapter. She calls all who lead and influence our youngest learners to do so with a solid knowledge base of what these students and their teachers require to thrive in our schools. My mantra as an educator of the young is, "To educate them in such a way that their foundation is so firmly established that there will never be an opportunity for even a sliver of a gap to develop during all of their years of schooling." Jessica writes with this mindset of responsibility and commitment for every young student! For this, I am honored to call her both a friend and colleague. She has written a must-read book for all who influence the education of our youngest learners."

HEIDI VEAL
EARLY CHILDHOOD LITERACY AND PROGRAMS ADMINISTRATOR,
LEWISVILLE ISD

"Today's generation of modern learners will enter a world of work that is vastly different than the one our school leaders entered not too long ago. If we are going to transform teaching and learning, we must do so, starting in the earliest grades. The acceleration of technology, new research, and new standards continue to push the envelope for all in our pre-K–12 system, and the earliest years lay the foundation for our students' future success. In *Hacking Early Learning*, Cabeen shares stories, solutions, and practical strategies that can be implemented tomorrow in schools."

THOMAS C. MURRAY
DIRECTOR OF INNOVATION, FUTURE READY SCHOOLS,
CO-AUTHOR OF *LEARNING TRANSFORMED: 8 KEYS TO DESIGNING TOMORROW'S SCHOOLS, TODAY*

"This easy-to-read book serves as not only an excellent road map to leading at the PK-3 level, but reassures principals, who likely were not prepared in their initial licensure programs, that learning is for the leaders too. Cabeen lays out research-based, common sense approaches to creating the learning environments our youngest learners and their families deserve."

DR. KATIE PEKEL,
UNIVERSITY OF MINNESOTA PRINCIPAL IN RESIDENCE

"More than a book, *Hacking Early Learning* is a personal blueprint for anyone working with our youngest learners. Jessica Cabeen takes the research we've known about for years and illuminates how to help students succeed by the end of their third-grade year. Much like glitter and glue sticks, this is a book you'll want to read and have to read. It will cement your understanding of how to teach and reach the students who are counting on you the most."

DR. BRAD GUSTAFSON
NATIONAL DISTINGUISHED PRINCIPAL AND BEST-SELLING AUTHOR

"Jessica is one of the most passionate and dedicated educators I know. Having had the opportunity to actually visit her school in Minnesota, I've seen firsthand how her 'hacks' have transformed the learning and educational environment for her staff and students. *Hacking Early Learning* gives you tangible advice and resources to move your system forward, and it is a MUST-read book!"

ADAM WELCOME
DIRECTOR OF INNOVATION AND TECHNOLOGY,
CO-AUTHOR OF *KIDS DESERVE IT!* AND AUTHOR OF *RUN LIKE A PIRATE!*

"*Hacking Early Learning* is a must-read for educators and school leaders of our youngest learners. So much of education focus is on increasing rigor, standards and high-stakes testing accountability, which has inadvertently left out what is necessary for our littlest learners. Often, principals find themselves in the role of leading a school that includes our youngest grades, including Kindergarten and/or preschool, yet have no experience in those grades and may have misconceptions about what is happening during "play time" or how to handle student behaviors at that age. *Hacking Early Learning* will take the research into action for you as you read the innovative work at Cabeen's school. You will gain practical ways to lead your littlest learners while having high levels of learning for all."

JESSICA JOHNSON
PRINCIPAL, CO-AUTHOR OF *THE COACH APPROACH TO SCHOOL LEADERSHIP*

"Jessica's work should be shared with every school in the country. Her writing highlights the importance of being intentional when it comes to our youngest learners. The hacks challenge readers to think beyond boxed curriculums; exposing our students to innovative practices that will prepare them for the future. This book proves that innovation, play, and collaboration have a place in every school. If you want students to be excited about school, this is a must-read for you."

LYNMARA COLON
PRINCIPAL/LEAD LEARNER, MARY WILLIAMS ELEMENTARY

"In your hands is a book that will challenge you to "level up" your leadership game. Jessica Cabeen is revolutionizing early childhood education as the principal of the Woodson Kindergarten Center.
Each week in the mastermind, I have the privilege to learn from Jessica and "hack" her brain for school leadership insights. Now, she has literally written the book on how early childhood education should be approached. I have long admired her accomplishments and can't wait to hear how this book impacts school leaders around the world."

DANNY "SUNSHINE" BAUER
HOST OF THE #1 DOWNLOADED PODCAST FOR SCHOOL LEADERS,
BETTER LEADERS BETTER SCHOOLS

"This book flat-out champions early learners and the schools which serve them. It is the perfect combination of theory and practice. Principal Cabeen's writing is honest and sincere with each chapter providing thought-provoking research along with her proven professional insight. *Hacking Early Learning* is a must-read for all educators no matter what age group they lead."

JUSTIN HOLBROOK
FOURTH-GRADE TEACHER,
BALTIMORE CITY SCHOOLS' 2017 TEACHER OF THE YEAR

"Jessica Cabeen's hacks address the most pressing issues faced by early childhood education leaders today. Like Jessica, most administrators do not have an early childhood background, and if that is you, her story will inspire you! If you desire to learn from someone who is breaking every mold and transforming early childhood education across the county, this book is a must-read."

NANCY ALVAREZ
PRINCIPAL, CELINA PRIMARY SCHOOL

"*Hacking Early Learning* is a highly accessible read that frames the urgent need to focus on early learning as a foundation for all levels of learning. Jessica includes high-impact, actionable tips for enriching the learning experience in the early years. These tips are accessible and extra-mile hacks that will no doubt have broad impacts on the learning culture within the building as well as community. Jessica's experiences and servant leadership that engage all stakeholders and a whole community are inspirational and completely doable for all learning leaders."

SARAH JOHNSON
FORMER PRINCIPAL, SPOONER HIGH SCHOOL

"In *Hacking Early Learning*, Cabeen dives into the various building blocks that have made her school successful. Her ideas are practical and replicable; her voice is passionate; and it's easy to see why Cabeen's work is making a difference across the country. If you're looking for a Pre-K–3 book to help you to infuse into learning new ideas that consider the whole child, look no further."

ROSS COOPER
PRINCIPAL, OLD TAPPAN SCHOOL DISTRICT,
AUTHOR, APPLE DISTINGUISHED EDUCATOR,
GOOGLE CERTIFIED INNOVATOR

"As someone who had spent most of his career as a secondary teacher and administrator, I was a bit nervous when I became an elementary principal with an attached preschool on my campus. I consider myself blessed to have educators like Jessica Cabeen in my PLN who have been so instrumental in sharing their lessons learned and best practices to ensure the success of others. What impresses me most about *Hacking Early Learning* is that the hacks Jessica suggests are ones that can impact educational leaders at all levels of pre-K–12 schooling. Whether it be leading professional development the way you want students to learn or putting play back in the school day, I have seen the impact these hacks have not only had at Jessica's school but my school as well. *Hacking Early Learning* is a must-read for all school leaders who want to ensure their students develop a strong foundation of a love for learning, and I will be sharing it with all of my teachers as well as other site and district leaders."

DR. TODD SCHMIDT
PRINCIPAL, HARBOR VIEW ELEMENTARY

HACKING
EARLY LEARNING

HACKING
EARLY LEARNING

10 Building Blocks to

in

That **ALL** Teachers and School
Leaders Should Know

Jessica Cabeen

PUBLICATIONS

Hacking Early Learning

© 2018 by Times 10 Publications

These books are available at special discounts when purchased in quantity for use as premiums, promotions, fundraising, and educational use. For inquiries and details, contact us at www.hacklearning.org.

Published by Times 10
Highland Heights, OH
Times10Books.com

Project Management by Kelly Schuknecht
Cover Design by Najdan Mancic
Interior Design by Steven Plummer
Editing by Carrie White-Parrish
Proofreading by Jennifer Jas

Library of Congress Cataloging-in-Publication Data is Available.
ISBN: 978-1-948212-02-1
First Printing: March, 2018

TABLE OF CONTENTS

FOREWORD

Jessica Cabeen is a highly respected colleague who has become an integral member of my professional learning network (PLN). Over time, she has also become a friend. That said, the invitation to write this foreword isn't a favor, but an honor. Before I go any further in highlighting why Jessica is one of education's up-and-coming leaders/practitioners, I am compelled to provide you with important information that will help you decide if you've made a worthwhile purchase. All too often, I find myself too far into a book when I realize it isn't delivering on what it promised or on what I need. I am providing you with critical information up front, so that you'll know before you read the first word of the first chapter whether this book is going to deliver... and whether you're ready for what it definitely delivers.

Have you ever stopped to notice those commercials boasting about some new pharmaceutical breakthrough? They show a new miracle medicine that has as its backdrop the misery of the person's life "before," and then an amazing burst of energy, vigor, and opportunity in the same person after taking the new miracle drug. Admittedly, some of the "after" imagery is so attractive that I find myself considering an order—even when I don't have any of the symptoms or conditions the drug was designed to treat. You'll be pleased to learn that I've never gotten as far as picking up the phone, because just as I squint to focus on the tiny numbers on my cell phone, the lightning-fast, tongue-twisting disclaimer begins. This is where we learn of the drug's four hundred and seventeen potential side effects, all four hundred and seventeen communicated in under thirty seconds. Thirteen of the side effects are worse than death. By the time the commercial's talented speed talker is done reading off the list of maladies, I've placed my cell phone back on the nightstand. So, what's the point of all this, you ask?

Well, the foreword of a book is located close to the front cover, and typically can be read before the binding of a book has been broken to the point of no return. With that in mind, I want to provide a speed-spoken list of disclaimers that will help you decide whether you should continue reading this book, return it for a refund, or gift it to a colleague. Consider it a public service from yours truly.

On the other hand, if you believe in your mind, body, and soul that educators have an opportunity on a daily basis to leverage an amazing level of impact on our youngest learners, then get ready to add this book to your arsenal.

I have the great honor and privilege to live my life's work on a daily basis. I travel across all parts of North America, delivering long- and short-term professional development conferences, workshops, and keynote addresses. My work affords me the opportunity to connect with tens of thousands of educators on an annual basis. As you can imagine, there are some educators who stand out. At the beginning of our connection, I regarded Jessica as one who had knowledge of the right work, could communicate the right work, and always seemed to say the right things. But you know as well as I do that there are many who can say the right things.

The real test comes in regard to whether they *do* the right things.

Well, in the summer of 2017, I had the incredible opportunity to witness firsthand Jessica's leadership at work. I spent a day with her staff, and what I witnessed, examined, analyzed, and experienced couldn't be staged. There was no way she could've orchestrated a dog and pony show. Because not only was the culture of high levels of learning for ALL palpable, there was meaningful data to support it.

Moreover, Jessica's professed culture of "high levels of learning for ALL" was clear in the way she was able to sit back and allow her staff to communicate and respond to my questions and queries. Jessica embodies this culture, and has skillfully and intentionally empowered her staff to embody it as well. The most effective leadership is exhibited when an established culture is able to THRIVE in the leader's absence. If Jessica decided to run for President of the United States in 2020 (she'd have my vote), I'm confident that the culture on which her school feeds will continue to grow and evolve over time—even without her.

A mentor to both Jessica and me, Becky DuFour, often said, "You don't have to be mean to mean business." Jessica is that kind of leader. She is relational by nature; a natural coach and connector. It doesn't take long to feel safe and supported by her. All too often, we regard this level of connection and high expectations for execution of collective commitments as mutually exclusive. This is not the case with Jessica. It's clear what comes first, and that is doing what's best for kids. In second place is supporting and comforting adults. But to be clear—it's a distinct second place. I grew and evolved into the same kind of leader, so I both recognize it when I see it, and know it can pay great dividends. There is no more powerful combination than expecting the best and knowing how to coach adults during the journey.

I learned a ton about what we can expect from our earliest learners. What struck me most is that everything they're implementing at the Woodson Kindergarten Center can be implemented at every stage of learning throughout a student's K–12 matriculation. While I've never wavered from the belief in a staff's ability to ensure high levels of learning for all, I have no practical experience with day-to-day instruction. I was a school principal of a pre-K–5 school, but never taught in any of the primary grades as a classroom teacher. So to see this culture of excellence in action with kindergarteners stretched my thinking, and strengthened my resolve.

Lastly, I'll share what I believe will make this a slam-dunk book that will soon be mangled at the corners, stained with notes in the margins, and exhibit tabs protruding from its pages...

This is a book about a ton of NOTHING new ... and I LOVE that. And for that, Jessica should take a bow, because while there's nothing new in this book, the "new" in this book is in Jessica's ability to offer powerful nuance (new ... nuance, do you see what I did there?) for each principle.

So often in my travels, schools are looking for the next magic bullet, shiniest toy, latest piece of software, coolest app, or anything else that can be described as a fix. Now don't get me wrong, there's nothing wrong with innovation; my family calls me Gadget Man. The problem as I know it is that we look for fixes rather than executing the fundamentals with fidelity. We try something, and if it doesn't yield results, we either abandon the practice or initiative, pile on another initiative, or persist in grinding out the initiative so we can subconsciously have proof that it doesn't work, and sometimes have an excuse to revert back to ineffective practices.

The beauty of this book is in the nuances. I'll divide nuance into two categories: creases and blind spots. Creases represent those areas that reveal themselves when you look closely and press down on the corner of the couch cushions. Blind spots represent those things you learn once you've exhausted everything you know. Jessica takes the fundamental components of a culture of excellence and forces the reader to reflect on implementation and practice. In this book, she has a knack for climbing into the reader's head with one of three things:

1. A nuance associated with a practice that you hadn't considered (creases).

2. An aspect of implementation brought to the forefront of your mind's eye via a timely reminder (blind spots).

3. A feeling of validation about your current practice.

While there were times I certainly felt pride in validation, I spent more time vacillating between "Now that's something I hadn't thought of" (crease) and "Oh yeahhhhh, that's right! I hadn't thought of that possibility!"

This is the gold of *Hacking Early Learning*. This is the sweet spot. This book is built for speed regarding how quickly you can implement and adjust, and built for action because it's written by a powerful practitioner with boots on the ground.

The bottom line is that Jessica and the team at Woodson invest more belief in their ability to ensure high levels of learning for ALL students than anything else. Before they open a folder, read a file, or examine one set of data about a student, that collective confidence is in place. They see themselves as the baddest cats on the planet, up to the task of meeting every challenge that creates the path between where a student is and where a student needs to be. They have kindergarteners coding, for heaven's sake! This seemingly small shift in thinking has produced seismic results. They value culture over comfort—and you will see and feel that as you move through this book.

—KEN WILLIAMS, CHIEF VISIONARY OFFICER, UNFOLD THE SOUL

INTRODUCTION

Rethinking learning in the early years

"Hello, my name is Jessica, and I am a recovering middle school assistant principal."

WHAT DO YOU remember about kindergarten? For me it was a half-day program a few days a week, a lot of play, and included a nap. If you work in a pre-K to third-grade setting, you know that what I just described is no longer what learning in the early years looks like in our schools. Academic expectations, teacher preparatory programs, parent involvement, technology, and students' social and emotional learning have completely reshaped the world, and how we learned is no longer how we should teach. The concern now is how we adjust to that change in practice.

Some of today's schools have kept early learning the same as it was before, naps and all, but are lacking the vertical alignment to academic expectations in the third- through 12th-grade years. Other schools went all the way to the other side of the pendulum. Desks in rows, worksheets, and little bodies trying to learn in ways that are not developmentally appropriate, and not successful for most. There is no fault or blame placed on where you fit most; we all have much to learn when it comes to setting the right academic, behavioral, and social-emotional expectations for learners from age three to eight.

Today, we are facing challenges in education that haven't been addressed before, and have an incredible opportunity to shape, inspire, engage, and empower our future school, community, and maybe even national leaders of tomorrow. The longer I lead in early learning the more I learn and grow myself. The research is clear, and it is available. What we need is a way to take that research to action.

As a "recovering middle school assistant administrator," I walked into my first year of leading in the early grades thinking I had what I needed to lead. Looking back now, I made mistakes, had assumptions, and misunderstandings in regard to developmentally appropriate practices for our youngest learners. After six years of listening and learning, though, I now understand the key indicators for leading students, staff, and families in the pre-K/K years, and guiding students to success all the way to their college and career years. My continued mission is to ensure that all students have the supports necessary to meet the success that they each deserve, and my passion is to support other educators in understanding—by any means necessary—the ways to support student success. *Hacking Early Learning* became a way to share this knowledge with others and develop a larger community of educators passionate about dreaming big for our littlest learners.

So why read this book? Do you want to make a big impact on our littlest learners? Are you interested in becoming an administrator, but have no clue what you would do if you were provided with an opportunity to lead at an elementary school? Have you been teaching or leading in the elementary grades for a while, and now want to try something in a different way?

We ask our students to take risks, make mistakes, and learn along the journey, and we as adults should take our own advice. So in true pre-K to third-grade fashion, here are some rules for reading *Hacking Early Learning*:

1. Play fair.

In each of these sections, I will give a little background research into why we are doing what we are doing. If this is a new area of learning for you, I will suggest further resources for you to dive into, both in the book and at jessicacabeen.com. Just like in a game of kickball at recess, you really need to learn the rules before you play.

2. Be nice.

While reading this book, you might want to ask other educators more about a topic, or how they are providing supports to students. Please be mindful that some of us have been doing what we have been doing for a really long time, and will need gentle conversations if you are suggesting changes in practices. Choosing to teach in the early grades is a commitment not only in educational practice, but emotional patience, and takes much heart. Educators at these grades are not just teachers by title, but by their whole hearts and souls, so feedback is far more personal than you might think.

3. Ask for help.

Just like learning to tie your shoe for the very first time, you'll need to see examples, take time to practice, and have friends to help you along the way. Make a commitment to reach out to another school site, become more connected in your state/national organizations, and/or find a PLN via social media that will help you grow in your understanding.

4. Never stop learning.

Fair warning: Entering into this work is like introducing finger paint to a class for the very first time. It will be messy, it won't be perfect, but you will have learned and created something at the end that you should really be proud of trying.

By reading this book, you are jumping into an exciting journey to becoming a stronger educator for our young learners. I look forward to having you be a part of this richly diverse tribe, which has a passion to ensure that all early learners have high expectations and resources for their current and future success. I hope you find your own inspiration, ideas, and hacks for early learning in the pages ahead!

DREAM BIG FOR OUR LITTLEST LEARNERS!

Creating high expectations, no excuses pre-K through third grade

"Leaders who love their work are always learning."
—ERIC SHENINGER AND THOMAS MURRAY, *LEARNING TRANSFORMED*

THE PROBLEM: KINDERGARTEN IS NOT THE NEW FIRST GRADE

WE HAVE A pivotal role at a critical time in education. For many years, early learning was a luxury—a fun thing for little learners. Now, more research is indicating what educators already knew: that early learning is the most important learning. Research-based strategies that are implemented well can reduce achievement gaps, gain positive family relationships, decrease truancy, increase engagement, and provide a healthy, successful start from cradle to career.

For this reason, leading a classroom, leading a school, or leading within a district provide challenges and opportunities every day. In the world of early learning, those days are broken up into minutes of intentional opportunities to educate and empower the future of a child. But what if you are walking into a new school or a new grade level, and lack background experiences with this new setting? Every second we as adults play catch-up to the learning we needed to do earlier, we are losing time to impact the students in our class.

 **Our students are changing, and the outcomes are more rigorous at a younger age, but our instructional practices are staying the same. We need to be the change. Getting it right from the beginning is critical for the future successes of all students.**

The research is clear: Quality early learning programs significantly impact the long-term educational opportunities for all students in America. Historically, there has been a greater focus on third through 12th grades, rather than on pre-K–3. More recent research, legislation, and, well, common sense, have shifted that focus to the importance of quality preschool and kindergarten programs. Research supports the work of closing the achievement gap before it starts in the K–12 world. Ensuring that school leadership is equipped with knowledge of pre-K–3 is a key factor in supporting high-quality early learning environments in schools.

With principal licensure programs more geared toward the third- through 12th-grade setting, there is a need for practical advice from leaders living in the pre-K–3 world every day. From decreasing retentions and referrals to special education, to improved student achievement and graduation rates, the research is clear: Quality pre-K/K is no longer nice, but necessary for all students to have access to in the United States. Our job today is to take the research and apply it to our classrooms tomorrow.

While kindergarten expectations are ramping up, the developmentally appropriate learning environments are evaporating at a rapid pace. This, paired with college programs licensing K–6 educators, with minimal time in the pre-K/K, is setting the stage for a lack of hands-on experience for new teachers entering our schools. This puts schools in a position to continue to drill down instructional practices that work well in the upper grades, but have no place in pre-K through third grade.

My personal connection to disrupting assumptions and elevating expectations in the early years occurred when I became a principal at the school where my son would have his first school experience. He lived in Ethiopia until he was five and a half years old, and while he entered the education system well below all defined bars, he continued to exceed academic and behavioral outcomes as he moved through the grades. My mission for his success became a passion for finding ways for *all* to succeed, regardless of barriers or preconceived notions of abilities.

Our students are changing, and the outcomes are more rigorous at a younger age, but our instructional practices are staying the same. We need to be the change. Getting it right from the beginning is critical for the future successes of all students. Creating developmentally appropriate learning spaces and supporting instructional practices with teachers are the pathway to this success.

THE HACK: DREAM BIG FOR OUR LITTLEST LEARNERS

The more time you invest in understanding the connections from when children are born until they are college bound, the better you can support all stakeholders. This support can look like enhancing student learning experiences by investing in quality play-based instructional time every day. Supporting teachers might include embedding high-quality professional development that meets the developmental needs of working with early learners. Including parents as partners in their child's first few years of school might look like including social media as a part of your school message, and as a way to show parents what you do each and every day. Regardless of what you do to enhance your school, it has to start with a solid focus and mission.

Establishing a school mission or mantra is one thing. Finding ways to measure, monitor, and involve all stakeholders in the success of the school mantra is the deep work we need to focus on in schools today.

Too many times, leaders uncomfortable with the early years defer to the individual judgment of early learning classroom teachers to do what they think is right. This increases the risk of students having inconsistent expectations and learning experiences between teachers and across grade levels. While allowing teachers the ability and opportunity to share their vision for their students is terrific, a leader still needs to be driving the bus. When you work as a team to understand the needs of learners, and create the learning outcomes that will be consistent across all teachers, you are able to build a consistent path toward success for all.

Once you have a deeper sense of the multiple facets of early learning and the connections to learning, it is time to start on the journey. Find time for your team to take that research into practical application in your school setting—it's essential if you want to ensure that there are consistent high expectations, and that those expectations are understood by all stakeholders. Start simple: What is the one thing that you feel has to be tackled first? If you have high suspension rates in the early grades, consider building a framework for consistent behavioral expectations building-wide, with a lens of understanding the developmental needs of students who are entering school for the first time. If you receive feedback from the intermediate and middle schools, saying that students enter with inconsistent academic vocabulary, work with your elementary teachers to establish essential outcomes and ways to monitor these through common formative assessments.

A road map is essential to staying on course with these big intentions and dreams. Too often, educators revert back to practices that are comfortable, instead of risking new practices that might not work out perfectly the first, second, or third time. But creating a framework with all stakeholders, implementing the practices, and monitoring the success are essential in moving pre-K through third-grade research to application in your school.

WHAT YOU CAN DO TOMORROW

- **Create a personal course of action.** Whatever knowledge you are coming into this work with, it is important to create a plan that covers three things: what you know for certain, what you are unsure of, and what you want to know more about. Use a tool such as the NAESP *Leading pre-K–3 Learning*

Communities or Kauerz and Coffman's *Framework for Planning, Implementing, and Evaluating PreK–3rd Grade Approaches* to build a full picture of what quality pre-K through third-grade programming entails. From that point, determine what area of early learning interests you the most, and focus on that concept first. Research ideas from books, blogs, and Twitter chats, and connect with others in the field. The more you learn and include in your plan, the more the students you serve will grow.

- **Shadow a student.** In order to understand early learning, I suggest you start with the experts first— the students. Take a full day to immerse yourself in a day in the life of an early learner. From breakfast to brain breaks and everything in between, put your computer away and just engage in the day-to-day of a student in pre-K or an early grade. At the end of the day, take twenty minutes to reflect on what you saw, and create a list of things that you are wondering about, and what you want to learn more about. The list might include things such as explicit teaching of social-emotional skills, open-ended questions during play time, groupings of students during math/reading centers, and the management of transition time. As a leadership team, these lists can become the start of practice profiles, or documents that align key early learning practices across grade levels, and provide all educators consistent look fors and ways to assess implementation of strategies.

- **Shadow an educator.** On a different day, and if possible a different class setting, spend time watching a day from the view of the classroom teacher. Take time to observe the intentional interactions every moment during the day. From supporting students resolving an issue outside of the bathroom to asking high-level questions during a small-group reading time, you will see the teacher demonstrating exemplary practices that you can draw from, grow, and build on—all using the expertise of other teachers. When the observation is over, make sure to thank the educator for the time. This exercise is a way for you to deepen your understanding of key instructional practices needed in the early grades, while honoring the time and dedication teachers put into this work.

- **Develop a comprehensive plan with a team.** Now that you have a deeper sense of the work ahead of you, it is time for your team to take that research into practical application. Make a list of what you feel has to be tackled first. Using the example from the last section, if you're experiencing high suspension rates, put that at the top of the list and decide how you'd like to deal with it. If you're receiving feedback from upper-grade teachers about your students' vocabulary, put that on the list, along with a list of possible appropriate solutions. Use what you've learned from shadowing students and teachers to come up with solutions that you think will work best.

A BLUEPRINT FOR FULL IMPLEMENTATION

Step 1: Find out why people believe in this work.

Take time to talk about your school's goals through the lens of every stakeholder in the school, to ensure that all have a way to see themselves in the work ahead. For example, ask people what they think every student should know and be able to do before they enter the next grade, to give yourself a broader perspective of people's knowledge, understanding, and passion. This simple question-and-answer segment will give you deeper insight, and address misconceptions. Early learning educators invest in their work because it is a deeply personal calling, which can be based upon their personal experiences, the experiences of their own children, or their years of teaching. Capturing their stories in your school's goals will ensure that they stay committed to helping all students prepare for third grade and beyond.

Step 2: Create collective commitments that everyone can get behind.

Once you know the why, it is time to get to the how of the work. Establish a set of collective commitments (as outlined below in

Image 1.1) as the ground rules for the work ahead. For example, if your mantra or mission is "high expectations, no excuses," develop collective commitments as stepping stones to the mission. When you spend time in classrooms, make a point to ask about those commitments, to gain stakeholders' opinions in an authentic and trusting setting. Whatever is decided needs to become the school's guiding ground rules. Have everyone sign them, and then post them and review them weekly. That way you know that students are receiving the same guidance in every room in your school—and that consistency will help to prepare them for future success.

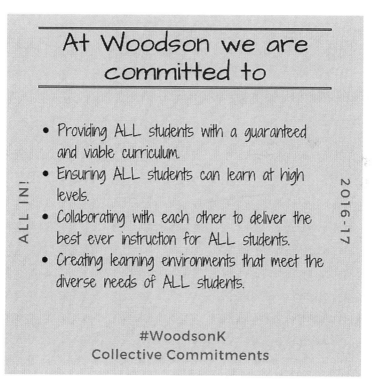

At Woodson we are committed to

ALL IN!

- Providing ALL students with a guaranteed and viable curriculum.
- Ensuring ALL students can learn at high levels.
- Collaborating with each other to deliver the best ever instruction for ALL students.
- Creating learning environments that meet the diverse needs of ALL students.

2016-17

#WoodsonK
Collective Commitments

Image 1.1

Step 3: Post them, but don't forget about them.

We have all been in a school that has beautifully designed missions, site plans, and goals that are reviewed at the start of the school year and then lost, forgotten, or changed during the year without input. Regardless of your title, as an educator passionate about raising the bar for all students, you have an obligation to stay the path, rather than allowing it to change.

After gaining input from school stakeholders and setting the collective commitments for the school, create the goals that will drive you to the destination. Consider limiting yourself to three to four goals annually. Review them throughout the year, align professional development with them, monitor progress, and seek feedback on how your implementation is going.

Watch out for potholes during the year, too. For example, if a new initiative or workshop comes across your desk and isn't aligned with your goals, pass on it. Learning to say no to things that aren't directly aligned to your work isn't always an easy thing to do, but it is necessary.

Step 4: Stay the course.

The harder it gets, the better it becomes. Teaching in the early years is as challenging as it is rewarding. Each year, you start again—but with a little more experience and knowledge under your belt. Because the students are so young, the learning is large. It can be easier to retreat from new practices when the work becomes difficult, the push-back frustrating, and the data not exactly where you thought it would be. But work together, reminding each other why you are doing what you are doing, and that the benefits down the road will make it worthwhile.

Step 5: Increase communication about what you are doing and why.

When you are documenting, reviewing, reflecting, and celebrating the data and results, don't forget about external stakeholders. Find time to explain what, why, and how you are enhancing learning experience for your earliest learners. This enhances the opportunities for your mission to be understood, shared, and celebrated by others.

Do the high school principal and teachers know how much heavy lifting early learning educators are doing to prepare young learners for their high school years? Do local businesses know the importance of getting books into children's hands, even before they start kindergarten? And if they do, could they help by donating books or money, so you could create more community libraries by apartment complexes and community parks? Could your local library host a "Ready for K" night, where you could help parents through the enrollment process and explain how they can prepare their children for kindergarten, right from their home? When you intentionally share data outside of the four walls of the school, you invite others to celebrate, support, and partner with you on what you are trying to accomplish.

OVERCOMING PUSHBACK

While you are gaining this new information, remember that creating detailed courses of action and changing the course for your school might not be a trip to Disney World. Creating a course of action and collective commitment means just that: We are all in, the whole school, all the stakeholders. But building the buy-in necessary to make change won't come without bumps along the road. Here are some possible arguments—and some responses for you to use.

It might not work right away. When we're making significant changes to curriculum, social-emotional supports, and parent involvement, it is easy to agree in August, but sometimes hard to follow-through in January. Review the processes and protocols set at the start during times of resistance and change, so that you don't undermine the work you have already done. Mistakes, or implementation failures, are just opportunities to review processes and make small changes to the larger plan.

It's too frustrating to try new things. Be careful that frustration doesn't take over, and take out a new idea or initiative. If a new behavior system isn't working, go back and review how students are reminded about checking their self-regulation. Are visuals posted around the school as cues for students and adults? When you're problem-solving the issue of a student's ability to stay engaged in learning, who calls the parent and asks the key developmental questions and strategies that they have used successfully? Establish leadership teams to help monitor and address small missteps before they turn into bigger mistakes. These teams can also help hold each other accountable by creating norms and setting key goals to focus on during the year.

Does it even matter? Switch the order of two words in the statement above to completely change what is being said. Collecting data that is relevant, understood, and meaningful can be a complex challenge in the early years. Sitting twenty-five five-year-olds down in September to administer a fill-in-the-bubble standardized assessment will never give anyone a true picture of the gifts, talents, and skills each child brings to a class. Instead, help educators, administrators, and community members understand the importance and relevance of informal, developmentally appropriate assessment measures and their connections to learning in later grades. Find ways to show student data, and share that data early on, to create the sense of ownership and responsibility needed for buy-in to the early grades.

There's not enough time to network with other administrators. The work described in this hack isn't easy, and certainly doesn't have an immediate return on investment (some of these students still have thirteen years of school before they graduate). But the time spent on the work, along with the opportunities to collaborate with others, will be immeasurable. Find accountability partners internally and externally, to help you stay on course. Join in on a Twitter chat that is relevant to an area of early learning of interest to you. At a staff meeting, share learning from a recent conference, seek other educators to jump into a book relevant to early learning with you, or invite a colleague to attend a conference with you. Find ways to interact—so that you can all grow and succeed.

There's not enough time to network with other teachers. Observe teachers who exemplify key strategies, and match teachers up together, to give everyone a chance to see the theory in practice and ask questions. Our probationary teachers are assigned mentor teachers, based upon the skillsets of both educators. New teachers are also supported by our instructional coach, who not only observes the teacher, but subs for the new teacher so that teacher can go into classes of master teachers to see the work in action.

These observations also allow master teachers a chance to reflect on their own practices, and share resources with others. No other classes for a teacher to observe in your school? No problem. These can be done in person or creatively through Google Hangouts or Skype.

THE HACK IN ACTION

Our mantra for our school is "The happiest place in Southeastern Minnesota." Parents and visitors comment on how polite and happy everyone is when they come to visit, substitute teachers appreciate how helpful other teachers are and how welcoming the office staff is, and students love the morning dance parties and High-Five Fridays as a way to roll out the red carpet for learning as they walk into school. Our thought was if students walked into the building happy and excited to learn, teachers and support staff felt encouraged to take risks, and parents felt welcome whenever they came to our school—we would have the foundation to create a school with high expectations, no excuses, and a fail forward attitude toward learning.

Behind that mantra, however, was an extensive road map that all stakeholders could see themselves in. Alignment, communication, and accountability are themes woven throughout everything we do. At the kindergarten center, we have weekly PLC meetings and review data from the school-wide common formative assessments created in reading and math. Teachers, specialists, and support staff work each week to find ways to extend, remediate, and review lessons to ensure that all students fully understand concepts before they move on to the next one. Our staff lounge has up-to-date percentages so that all stakeholders (teachers, paraprofessionals, custodial, office, and cafeteria staff) know where we are right now in the journey, and what we want all students to know before they go to first grade. As a school, we monitor academic and social-emotional outcomes with various formal and informal methods that are shared back to all stakeholders on a monthly basis. We have leadership committees that address concerns or questions that arise based upon data. And our professional development is created based upon the three aims of our site plan.

Just like with teaching, when leading with adults, every second counts, and we work as a collaborative team to provide meaning to everything we allow and everything we do in our school.

Finding other people to talk with about challenges and frustrations through the journey is critical for sustaining those high expectations through the rough spots. These should be people in your school, and outside. This advice was best demonstrated the year we eliminated the behavior clip charts from our school. While we knew the research behind why they were an ineffective tool, and felt it was the right choice, we were all frustrated at their absence by November. It would have been easy to return the behavior clip charts to the classroom walls—but it would have been the wrong solution. Instead, we kept pushing forward, asking specific questions of each other about what wasn't working, and trying new strategies for the students who continued to need more reminders than the rest when it came to classroom expectations. Our RtI (Response to Intervention) team scheduled more meetings and set time aside for classes that had significant behavioral challenges, to look at creative classroom supports. The PBIS (Positive Behavioral Intervention and Supports) team kept looking for new articles and resources that supported our initial reasoning for removing the clip charts, while encouraging other teachers to try new solutions to old behavior. Many of us reached out to our PLN on Twitter, Facebook, and Pinterest, and listened to podcasts that helped us understand other perspectives.

In the end, we have continued work to do, but we are working to find the answers together. Creating the action plan, investing the time, and working through the rough spots is not an easy thing to navigate. However, observing in classrooms, working with teachers, and listening to parents in the community to help solve those problems is completely worth the investment.

My learning in this work comes from many mistakes. My own assumptions of the expectations in the early ages impacted what I thought students should know and be able to do. I had no understanding of the workings of our district or community preschool programs. Leading and learning about the early years is about more than just research articles; it is about getting involved in the work.

People who visit our school always comment on how happy it is. However, establishing any school culture—and dreaming those big dreams for our little learners—takes time, energy, commitment, and input from all stakeholders.

LEAD FROM YOUR FEET, NOT YOUR SEAT

Becoming the visible leader your school needs

"If serving is beneath you, leading is beyond you."
—Anonymous

THE PROBLEM: TODAY'S LEARNERS DON'T NEED YESTERDAY'S LEADERS

For far too long, elementary, and more specifically, early childhood, leaders have been looked down upon. In the hierarchy of leadership positions, it almost looks like the opposite trajectory of a student's school experience. The most prestigious positions are those in central office, then high schools, middle schools, elementary schools, and then ... early childhood centers.

Principal licensure programs don't necessarily debunk this perception. Think about it: how many early childhood courses do you need to take to be a licensed principal at a pre-K–3 level? And if you're a secondary school teacher, when was the last time you observed, or taught, at a pre-K/K level to know what to look for or what to do?

When I walked into the Woodson Kindergarten Center, I was confident. During the six years leading up to that position, I was deep in the trenches of transition planning for post-secondary special education students, PBIS interventions at the middle school, literacy walkthroughs, and grading practice review. I mean how *hard* could kindergarten really be compared to leading at the middle/high school level? I was completely unprepared for what was to come.

Using your leadership position to get into the thick of it shows that all jobs are important, and ensures that all students have a positive start to the day. Your presence makes it a priority.

I was not at all prepared to be a strong leader in the early years. Any coursework or practical experience I had in the primary years was wiped away by my more recent middle and high school experience. Plus, to be totally honest, I was so far in age from my own kindergarten years that I didn't even know what to expect to see! How in the world was I going to lead in a place that I didn't have experience in teaching?

So how exactly do we go about leading in early learning—and respecting the position of leader to those early learning years?

THE HACK: LEAD FROM YOUR FEET, NOT YOUR SEAT

The answer is this: Stay out of your office. Staff, students, families, district leadership, and the local community's first impression of the school district is essential if you want to reflect the mission and vision of your school. And what that first impression looks like—well, that might surprise you. Because it starts and ends with the leader—and what that leader is *doing*.

Defining the role of leader at pre-K through third grade starts with redefining where the leader does the work. Leading the school from outside of your office—where the students are—shows everyone around you that you are ready and willing to help with the work. And in the world of early learning, everyone can always use an extra hand.

Using your leadership position to get into the thick of it shows that all jobs are important, and ensures that all students have a positive start to the day. Your presence makes it a priority. A few years ago, we were having some concerns with the parent drop-off space at our school, which was getting overly crowded. With some creative thinking, we created a drop-off lane for parents, where we would actually help the child get out of the car, so the parents could be on their way. During the initial start-up, I was out helping with traffic flow and looking for holes in our plan. And then I just... stayed. Each morning, for thirty minutes, I am out at student arrival. Rain, sleet, or snow, I love helping students out of the cars, greeting them off the bus, and saying hi to parents as they drop off and go. During the year, we change it up. On Fridays, I bring out our karaoke machine so students and parents can dance their way into the school. In December, we have a Salvation Army bell-ringing station, so we can model caring and giving toward others during the holiday season. And of course on Halloween, I am out directing traffic in full costume.

The important thing is that I'm out there leading—on my feet, rather than from my seat.

When I worked in middle school, we had assemblies in which a counselor would speak to the grade level in the assembly, and recognize the student of the month, and then kids would exit the auditorium and return to class. At Woodson, assemblies took on a whole new approach. As part of our SEL (social-emotional learning) work, we decided that our students needed a more interactive assembly for them to really understand the character traits we were overviewing and recognizing. The social worker set forth to create plays to perform for students. From *The Boy Who Cried Wolf* to a dramatic retelling of the book *The Big Hug*, I was transferred out of my role of reading student names at assemblies to dressing up and acting like a six-year-old boy, a little girl named after a flower, a stubborn big brother who didn't want to give up his little boy bed, or a crayon who was ready to take a leave of absence from his day duties. Students loved the plays! They were so engaged during the story, and talked about it for days after the assembly was over. Staff enjoyed seeing the principal act quite different in those opportunities. And the leader (deep breath) took a major risk—costume and all—every time she did one of them in the name of connecting with the students on a personal level, and equipping them with the very best learning opportunities possible.

Becoming a great leader also means learning about and engaging in classroom learning. Try to model learning practices alongside teachers whenever possible. During a class, read aloud and work with the students based on learning you've done yourself, in your PLC meetings. Taking professional development into direct teaching experiences and modeling the learning you are doing allows you to recognize teachers and the work *they* are doing for their classrooms, to provide high-quality learning experiences for all students.

Find opportunities to take the reins on teaching in big and small ways. Every November, I teach two twenty-five-minute music lessons a week, to prepare students for leading the holiday program in December. From February to May, I teach small groups of students in our school Coding Club. In both of the above examples, I find ways to weave strategies into my teaching to support and enhance learning targets. Finding ways to practice what I preach also allows me to gain a deeper understanding of what teachers are trying to teach every day—so I'm connecting not only with students, but with their teachers, as well.

WHAT YOU CAN DO TOMORROW

- **Start small and go from there.** Find a need in your school, and make a commitment to fill it. It might be morning playground supervision, or one grade level of lunch every day. Whatever it is, schedule it into your day and treat it like you would an important meeting. Building routines and finding ways to be visible and valuable in the work will benefit your school and help you to build relationships with those around you.

- **Tweet, tag, blog, or text.** Start a list to build on every day. Documenting your learning holds you accountable to the work, and also provides others with opportunities to see creative ways to fill a need each day. Using your own school hashtag or Twitter account is a great way to reflect on the week. In our Friday Focus, I include pictures from Twitter to highlight things that happened during the week, for everyone to see. If I need ideas for creative ways to be in classrooms, I look at the #PrincipalsinAction or #KidsDeserveIt hashtags to see what other leaders are doing to push themselves out of the office and into the school. Texting pictures to parents is a great way to showcase learning, and build relationships with parents and students.

- **Shadow another principal.** Find another leader you look up to, and ask to shadow him or her for a day or even an hour. This is an incredible way to build your PLN and find new ways to be visible during the school day. For inspiration, I once drove to the Twin Cities area and observed two of my mentors: Mark French (principalfrench.com) and Brad Gustafson (@ GustafsonBrad). While their demographics, size of school, and ages of students were different than my own, finding good practices—by great leaders—gave me great ideas, no matter what the context. I loved observing the interactions they had with staff and students—how they managed to be visible and con-nected while getting the other "stuff" in their day done, and their commitment to high expectations for all was seen in their actions, and interactions with others.

A BLUEPRINT FOR FULL IMPLEMENTATION

Step 1: Get to every class, every day.

In January of 2016, my friend Eric Ewald (@EricEwald_Iowa) introduced me to a Voxer challenge, and because of that, I started to visit every class, every day. And I haven't stopped. During the first thirty minutes of the school day, I stop into each class and offer a formal greeting. It ranges from "Good morning, Woodson critters" to "Welcome to school today, green frogs!" Students respond back in so many ways, smiles always included. Initially, I was concerned that my presence would deter from the learning in the classroom, but what I found was exactly the opposite! Students looked forward to my morning visits, and continued to complete their morning jobs in class. Some students would share something that happened the night before, some showed me learning they had already completed that morning, and others … well, they just needed a hug to start the morning.

Regardless of the need, as a leader, I look forward to these visits more than any other. They are daily opportunities to engage with school stakeholders, and ground me in our "why" every … single … day. They also help me to reframe any negative situations that may have occurred in my day, and give me a little space to be with the important people before I go back into the office and answer the emails/phone calls from other stakeholders.

Get into your classrooms. Interact with students and teachers. Make yourself a part of the team. Get out of that seat and onto your feet—and start leading those kids.

Step 2: Make instructional rounds.

After a year of implementation of PLCs, I was eager to get into classrooms regularly to see the work in action—and to validate the teachers in the new instructional practices they were digging into during professional development and flipped staff meetings. Using a format like the one from the Hall/Simeral book *Building Teachers' Capacity for Success: A Collaborative Approach for Coaches and School Leaders*, I started making rounds every day at Woodson. Initially, I wasn't sure what value I would have if I only visited each class for sixty to ninety seconds a day. Still, armed with a clipboard and my fitbit, I started visiting classrooms, boost-up/gym, play centers, greenhouse, indoor/outdoor recess, and the cafeteria, to back up my teachers.

These unscheduled visits allowed me to catch the greatness in the everyday moments of learning. I was able to watch peer-to-peer interactions and storytelling at the water table. I could observe a teacher strategically using elbow partners to work on understanding the meaning of a whole-group story. I watched one teacher execute a flawless transition between learning centers from her small-group reading table, without more than five words spoken.

And most important, I was able to see the intricate ways teachers set up learning to meet the needs of the students. In our *Friday Focus*, I highlight things I saw during the week, and I keep a spreadsheet for myself, so I can keep track of the different school environments I observe, and the types of learning I am seeing.

Get out into your school and start learning. You won't regret it—and it will help you build plans for the future.

Step 3: Enhance your street cred with teachers.

At first, when I started leading from my feet more than my seat, I was worried that the staff wouldn't appreciate the change. Boy, was I wrong. My school street cred went up substantially the moment I made myself visible, present, and engaged in the various school environments. Recognizing and jumping in when a class was down a paraprofessional and needed extra help during learning centers was a small gesture that made a big impact—and it will work for you every time. Spend time connecting with teachers after your observations, to ask questions that deepen your understanding, and to provide the teachers with opportunities to share in their joy of teaching.

By setting and showing my priorities of being in classrooms and working with kids, I have deepened the relationships with the other adults in the building. And it reminds me daily that my purpose and passion is not in a seat in the office, but on my feet throughout the school.

OVERCOMING PUSHBACK

What about my other work? Leaving your office for big parts of the day does mean that when you return, you'll have even more work waiting for you. And you can't exactly ignore that work. Before you start to shift from your seat to your feet, make sure you have a plan in place to address how to handle what happens when you are out of the office for long periods of time. To ensure that I don't fall behind on the other duties of leading, I have a twenty-minute meeting with the school secretary every day. We use that time to look at the week ahead, review budget, schedule meetings for teachers and staff evaluations, and take care of the other nuts and bolts of the job. When I am out in the building, she runs the office, takes the phone calls, and schedules meetings for me with staff when needed. By giving up the controls of my own calendar, I am able to take time to be out and about in the building.

Other people will judge me if they think I'm not doing my job. People who push the boundaries of traditional thinking or learning also have to deal with those who aren't quite there yet. It is easy to sink into negative feedback and pushback from people outside of the work, who might seek to diminish or distinguish the flame you are firing up in your school. When dealing with people outside of the organization, and comments that are the opposite of constructive, it is important to address things in a manner that is professional and highlights the work you are pushing forward. Lack of knowledge is generally the culprit of the barrier between two parties. "Kids play all day at your school" can be resolved by having the person come and observe play time and have a dialogue about the instructional outcomes of that playtime—along with research behind the benefits of play. Addressing things right away is critical to ensuring that the work you are trying to accomplish isn't sidetracked by the negative comments or actions of others.

People are going to ask where the principal is all the time. If you were a leader-from-your-seat-type principal, or you are now in a building where the former leader was always found in the office—and you aren't—it is important to clearly communicate with building stakeholders where you will be so they can find you. Since I've implemented these ideas, I've found that the staff are more comfortable finding me out and about if they have a quick question. Initially, though, I had to make sure to clarify how to find and communicate with me.

Using a *Friday Focus* to communicate your schedule for the next week helps people plan for your location, and also shows them what you value by your location. If people need to catch you for the "do you just have a minute" conversations, have them schedule that with the school secretary. Many times, I am caught in between classroom visits, and by the time I get back to the office, I have forgotten what the person an hour before asked. If they schedule a time, though, you can guarantee they will have your full attention, and be sure you are in a space and place to listen—and remember—what they are asking.

THE HACK IN ACTION

Leading early learners is not just about understanding the learning that is occurring in the building. It is about applying that knowledge by teaching students as well.

Being visible is critical, and not just for your current students and teachers. Andy Jacks, Elementary Principal (@_AndyJacks) in Prince William County, Virginia, knows that every moment counts. Andy's perspective changed when he experienced this himself as a parent. "I'll never forget a school visit years ago that made me realize this. I walked in during an open house and the principal just stared ahead and didn't even say hi or acknowledge me. I never forgot that moment and how I felt about that person as a leader."

At Andy's school, he makes sure that every family member that visits the office or attends events is made to feel like a valued member of the school community. He feels that this isn't limited to current students, either. Parents celebrate their pregnancies, proud that their future kindergarteners will be attending his school. He installed a Lego wall in the office so that little ones feel welcome and enjoy their visits with their siblings. Andy firmly believes that interactions with these future students are unique opportunities to build relationships and positive momentum so that by the time they attend as students, they are highly motivated and excited to be in school.

He also stresses the importance of being visible: "It is not always easy and you'll need to be on point every day, but these types of connections will change how you view your legacy."

Still, leading in the pre-K through third-grade level can really be the toughest job you will ever love. So as leaders, we need to take our commitment and work into the classrooms with—and for—teachers. While leading at Woodson, I have filled in for a few hours as a sub as needed, and handled the Coding Club and the holiday music program—all to lead from my feet. And I thought I was doing my best … until I was challenged by a teacher to get back into the classroom as a full-day sub for a teacher. Initially, I was a little nervous. A whole school day? What about email, meetings, discipline?

I was terrified.

Then I did it. I created a plan based on work from our school Site Team, and used it successfully. After that, I started rotating as a classroom teacher for entire days, in eighteen classrooms, over four months. From attendance to math centers and everything in between, I was in charge. Detailed sub notes were completed and left for me by the class's teacher, and I used every word of those notes. Plus, this day away from the class gave the teacher in question an opportunity to visit other classrooms, cover the office, and see the school from a different perspective for the day. Students loved having chances to show me what they knew, in a more intimate environment than my morning greetings or pop-ins during the day. They also asked some pretty interesting questions about what they thought I did all day, and most were surprised that I could read, teach math, and work a Smart Board as well.

It is easy to say "I understand" when speaking at a staff meeting, but until everyone sees you doing the work, "I understand" is hard to believe. Teaching in every classroom gave me the street credit I needed to help move our school forward in having high expectations for all learners—students, teachers, and principals included. The laughs I got at the last staff meeting when I explained how I opened up a whole-group discussion on a recent big book was deafening!

Leadership is not always about putting your most polished self forward. It is about showing your vulnerability, sharing a growth mindset with others, and having the ability to take risks.

To be a great leader, you need to be where the learning is occurring! Becoming a true school leader is not about looking the part—it is about doing whatever you must to meet the needs of your school. School leaders who spend their days in the office answering emails and phone calls aren't in the trenches, seeing the good, developing others, and sharing the great work with others inside and outside the school walls. They aren't leading from their feet.

Some days, being in and out so much can be exhausting. Supporting all stakeholders is a big job, and one that doesn't necessarily end when the school day is finished. But working with staff every day, and trying to be out and about, demonstrates the commitment toward learning that we want everyone to have. Knowing that is the expectation makes the work exciting and fulfilling.

USE ABCs, 123s, AND PLCs

Creating high-quality learning experiences and supports

"One of the most important jobs of a teacher is the translation of standards into classroom content."
—FIRSTSCHOOL: TRANSFORMING PREK-3RD GRADE FOR AFRICAN AMERICAN, LATINO, AND LOW-INCOME CHILDREN

THE PROBLEM: EARLY LEARNING HAS TO BE MORE THAN GLITTER AND GLUE STICKS

FINDING THE MIDDLE ground between play, learning outcomes, high-quality learning experiences, engaging lessons, assessment for learning, and content mastery can be like looking for a needle in a haystack. Just like our students, we can sometimes be distracted by the shiny new thing in front of us, and miss the big picture learning targets. I remember when I became a principal at the elementary level, and thought, *Wow, we have a good deal of fun here*. Special events are a huge part of the school culture at that level, from classroom to school-wide celebrations, and often include every student and staff member in a school.

But sometimes, with all that glitter, sparkle, and glue, we miss opportunities to make intentional connections to the day-to-day *learning*. Leading at this level requires holding all educators to high expectations—while understanding developmentally appropriate practices that align with grade-level outcomes. Leaving this up to teachers in isolation creates silos of learning and a disconnect between grade levels and expectations for each student. So leaders have to be active on these issues every day, to ensure that we are leading with the learner in mind.

Coming from the secondary level, I moved to elementary and found a whole new set of terms and vocabulary I needed to master. One of these was a thing called "Pinterest." So many teachers got so many great ideas from Pinterest every day, and shared these resources with other teachers to build their centers, decorate their bulletin boards, and create catchy notes home to families and students.

However, the problem with Pinterest (I run into this myself now, as well) is that it can suck you into a black hole of such cool and creative ideas that you lose sight of what you were looking for in the first place. Because this level has to be about more than the glitter and glue sticks. It has to be about learning as well. This journey has taught me something very important: We can still pin ideas and resources—but now we do so with a target in mind. Before looking for that next pin, work with educators to identify the learning targets they are attempting to reach with the activity. Alignment of everything we do in early learning is instrumental, because the time we have with these youngsters is short, and our opportunities to create sparks of engagement are instrumental in the rest of their learning careers. The art of teaching can be woven into the pedagogy in a systematic way when you have the clear vision and focus on what you are moving toward, and keep from getting caught up in the colors and construction.

THE HACK: USE ABCs, 123s, AND PLCs

Before you can agree on the learning outcomes you want to see, you need to have a clear and consistent understanding of what learning is needed. To start, you need to make sure everyone has a strong sense of the state-required outcomes, as a foundation to build upon.

When our school was challenged with creating a set of kindergarten readiness skills to share with parents and preschools, we first took the time to review what was currently available. As a team, we reviewed early learning outcomes from over ten states, and then surveyed preschool, kindergarten, and first-grade teachers to determine the top ten outcomes we should focus on. This process allowed us to take what was state-required, work to understand it at a deeper level, and then apply it to our local context.

After the readiness standards were finished, the fun started. Teachers took time to create "lessons" that parents, preschool teachers, and other people invested in early learning could teach. These lessons included materials you could find around the house or out in the community, for ease of implementation. We even invited community members to become "teachers," and created videos modeling how to teach the material. During our spring kindergarten readiness open house, all parents received a toolkit full of materials and videos that explained how to use them, as a way to enhance the opportunity to practice at home. By grounding ourselves in the right work first, we were able to use our creativity to develop lessons that were both fun and deeply connected to the learning.

Of course, it is one thing to create a set of essential outcomes, and an entirely different thing to monitor and support the learning of those tasks throughout the school year. Adopting the use of Professional Learning Communities (PLC) is a way to monitor the mastery of essential outcomes, support teachers in creating learning opportunities, and provide additional resources for remediation or extension of these concepts. The work starts by creating a PLC leadership team that meets monthly to review existing data, discuss the implementation of future common formative assessments, and navigate any hiccups along the way. As a grade-level center serving only kindergarten students, we are intentional about ensuring that we are preparing students for the grades to come. Our instructional coach is our connection to this vertical alignment. She often meets with the other four instructional coaches in the elementary schools to continue alignment conversations, and to make sure that we are preparing our over four hundred five-year-olds every year for the neighborhood elementary school they will be attending—with real knowledge, rather than just pretty decorations.

To become the best leader you can be, it's important that you find a way to follow this path yourself, and keep your young learners moving forward on the path to success by giving them the fullest possible learning foundation.

WHAT YOU CAN DO TOMORROW

- **Model what you want to see.** Becoming a great leader also means learning about and engaging in classroom learning. I try hard to model learning practices alongside teachers whenever possible. During classroom read-alouds, I attempt to stress concepts discussed in PLCs, and connect them to what a class is already working on (for example, in a recent read-aloud, students worked to identify whether the main character was near or far away from another character in the book). These are small but important steps in recognizing teachers and the work they are doing to provide high-quality learning experiences for all students.

  Make time to go into a class and observe, and then model your own actions after what the teacher is doing. Use this opportunity to build opinions about how it's working and what the teacher is teaching, and to brainstorm ideas to bring up in the next PLC meeting.

- **Work in collaboration and not isolation.** Ensuring that each teacher in a grade level is teaching the same expectations is critical as students move forward. When we were creating essential outcomes, this became dramatically apparent. The conversation was around retelling a story. After a discussion, the teachers realized that some were using "First, Next, Last" and others were using "Beginning, Middle, End" to aid in student retelling of the story. They realized that using different words to assess and teach students meant that they were setting those students up for inconsistency in future grades.

Take a moment and write down a list of possible inconsistencies across grades, to bring up at the next PLC meeting. Having a list prepared will help you lead a discussion that may bring other situations to light. Making sure you take the time to review what and how your school teaches and assesses students is just as important as the review of the results.

- **Celebrate successes big and small.** Mini celebrations are critical for the culture of the work. At least every six weeks, we call a full PLC (paraprofessionals are invited as well) to review the data walls, share celebrations, and ... well, breathe. The work of ensuring "All Means All" is rewarding, but exhausting at the same time, so making sure you honor that commitment and provide opportunities for rest and rejuvenation is critical.

Some of our celebrations have been as simple as having ice cream treats out on the lawn and reflecting on the initial implementation of Common Formative Assessments in math. One year, we rented a local art center and had an ugly sweater party, with holiday cookies, apple cider, and role-playing of student scenarios and what we could learn from them. The next time we had ice cream treats on the front lawn and shared our reflections of creating our first Common Formative Assessment through the use of a Thinking Map.

Map out your first mini celebration as a way of team building, and jot down some ideas. Find creative ways to take a brain break from the work and celebrate the successes thus far—and keep the list to add to as the ideas continue to come to you.

A BLUEPRINT FOR FULL IMPLEMENTATION

Step 1: Create a PLC leadership team.

Finding the right people for the team is the hardest, but most important job. Our leadership team is comprised of a teacher from each grade, the instructional coach, and initially a special education teacher. The team reviews rubrics, learns how to create norms, and develops strategies to navigate team discussions and conflicts. We continue to meet bi-monthly and rotate leadership members (one new person per year). This gives people the empowerment to lead discussions, create solutions, and work collaboratively to ensure that all students are learning at high levels. This team has to believe that ALL MEANS ALL—and that any failure of a student is our job to resolve, rather than the problem of the child.

Step 2: Get your data together.

Knowing where we are at the start offers us a clear path for getting through the school year. At our school, we use a variety of data sources. Prior to the start of the school year, we get data from preschool teachers, special education teams, and parents, as well as student observational data, and use that to make decisions on class placements. During our kindergarten registration, each student is assessed by a classroom teacher using our Common Formative Assessment in reading and math. This assessment data is used to inform class clustering, and also gives teachers a starting point for the class, well before the students even take their seats.

Find a method of gathering data that works for you, and gives you a good picture of where the students are when they enter your school year—and how you're going to best lead them toward the goals you're setting for them. Start with what feels right, and specialize your process as the years go by.

Step 3: Honor collaboration teams and time.

So you have the data ... now what? Without setting aside team time to review and discuss the data with teachers who are committed, creative, and passionate about holding all students to high expectations, you are going to struggle to reach all learners at high levels. PLCs meet weekly for one hour, with the agenda including fifteen minutes of "wine and cheese" (a chance to dump what happened that day), followed by a review of norms, and then a deeper dive into student progress on essential learning outcomes in reading and math. Make sure that your team is working together on solutions. During a recent PLC session, I listened in on a brainstorming discussion about a number of students struggling to follow three-step directions. One teacher offered up multiple reasons that this group might be struggling with this concept (it was the first few weeks of school, they had limited prior experience, they were in a new environment). The ELL (English language learners) teacher then offered up how assessing this concept would look on standardized assessments later in the year. That meant that all PLC members were working with the same understanding regarding the expectations we need to reach. After gaining the background information, the team went into specific ways they could reteach the skill, a discussion around setting up pre-academic skills such as cueing for listening/directional language, and ways in which they could reassess the student knowledge to determine whether a different intervention would be required. All of this information was written down and shared with everyone after the meeting—with timelines as to when the team would return to this data set in the future.

Creating time, space, and a framework to have these conversations allows teachers a chance to collaborate and dig deeper to support all students as they reach for those high expectations. Make sure that you set your teams up with the right resources—and then give them the space to use them, and each other, to get results.

Step 4: Document It!

Leading and learning in a grade-level center provides some unique challenges, one of which is ensuring that we are sending students to their elementary schools with a full picture of their academic and social gains, in a format that is accessible to teachers and principals. Much of our standardized and benchmark data is housed within our student information system, and the template we use to have parent conversations about student growth is consistent. This leads to accuracy of transitional academic data. Our behavioral data is parsed out at the end of the year, and shared with elementary teachers, along with transition sheets that paint a fuller picture of the progress students have made, and the strategies that teachers have put in place. These artifacts might include social stories, visual schedules, and even parent/school communication notebooks.

Find ways to document your students' paths through the year. What worked and what didn't? How did teachers approach the problems? What words were they using? It's important to document all of that, so that the information can travel with the students, for the best success. How do you decide whether something should be included? The litmus test for us was to ask if something was successful and would help the student continue to make social and academic gains in the next year. If the answer was yes, then we included it in the plan.

OVERCOMING PUSHBACK

My gut says this isn't working. None of my students know their letter sounds this year, and only a handful can count backward. What I am going to do? Well, are you looking at data, or are you using your gut? So many times, we assume and awfulize without having firm data to back up our statements. Using informal and formal data to identify your problems will help your team identify specific ways to intervene and support all learners.

I have to maintain different expectations for some learners. It happens a little at a time, and it isn't intentional. And it certainly isn't conscious. "They came from that side of town," or "They don't speak English at home," or "They didn't have preschool." These comments and conversations immediately lower the bar of high expectations and set the start of a gap of achievement—and are based upon obstacles rather than student-specific outcomes. As the leaders of pre-K through third grade, we need to model empathy over sympathy with our staff and students, to ensure that we continue to have high expectations and no excuses for anyone.

Having purposeful, intentional, and honest conversations around equity are critical to ensuring that our personal experiences are not negatively influencing our professional expectations. Just two weeks into becoming the principal of the kindergarten center, I received a call from a teacher who was working with my son in a kindergarten prep summer experience. "Jessica, Isaiah really struggled to stay in line today when we were going anywhere, and I am concerned he will start to wander around the building, so it is a safety issue as well," she stated. When I asked her what she said to him, not missing a beat, she said, "Isaiah, that cute face isn't going to work on me. Get back in line." And he did. Five years later, I remember that conversation and that teacher. She wasn't going to lower her expectations even a little bit for this student. Yes, he was new to the United States, and yes, he had lived through things many of us will never fully comprehend—but he still needed to become a successful, productive member of our society, and needed to be held to the same learning outcomes as any other student. Serving students from an empathic vantage point over a sympathetic one serves your whole class, and that specific student, by closing the opportunity and achievement gap well before third grade.

When there is alignment between learning outcomes and the creative measures educators take to enhance a student's experience in the lesson, the sky's the limit.

Early in my career, I learned from the middle school principal the value of the sheet cake conversation. When a teacher was using lower expectations or not pushing a student toward the high expectations they needed to be successful in sixth through eighth grade, she would ask, "Are you going to tell that parent that the decisions you are making today are going to negatively impact their opportunity to have a sheet cake at high school graduation later on in life?" Every decision, every action, impacts our students' future, no matter if it is in 12th or second grade. Leading with an eye toward the end game of graduation makes the decisions in between so much clearer.

I'm more comfortable just using worksheets. This is a critical point. Learning in the early years has to be engaging, and tap into the creativity each student possesses. This type of learning cannot be measured solely by the worksheets that come with a boxed curriculum, or those on teacher-created sites. Finding creative ways to teach and assess essential outcomes needs to be as varied as the students you serve. One of my favorite examples of the importance of creativity over boxed content is our science unit on engineering. A passionate group of teachers created the science curriculum we use at our school, and when it comes to the engineering unit, they decided to go big or go home. They pulled out all the stops. The unit is taught not only in the classroom, but also carried into the play center. Students create cars and ramps, and use marbles and tubes and any other materials they can find to test hypotheses. Teachers share extension materials so that parents can extend the learning to home, and students can't stop talking about this unit for weeks after it ends. This is just one of many examples of the work dedicated early educators can do to provide students with creative, open-ended learning experiences—and make it more fun than worksheets. When there is alignment between learning outcomes and the creative measures educators take to enhance a student's experience in the lesson, the sky's the limit. Trust me, I have seen the towers students built during that unit of study!

I don't know how to not unintentionally widen the gap. Without a set of consistent outcomes that all students should be able to do by the end of the school year, teachers might put the brakes on some of the essential learning. But that learning is something students need for foundational skills. And some of your students might be missing it. While working individually with students and documenting growth is appropriate, making all the students do the same work—possibly at a slower pace—is not. Use small groups, driven by classroom data, to focus on skills that need remediation and skills that could be extended. Students at any age should have opportunities to grow and learn at their own pace, with the adults offering support and guidance toward end-of-year outcomes.

THE HACK IN ACTION

One of Heidi Veal's (@VealHeidi) foundational mantras as an early childhood educator is "Let them be little." Having a career focused solely on educating our youngest learners has raised her awareness for providing the highest-quality schooling for them while remaining relentlessly dedicated to developmentally appropriate practices that honor their littleness. She states, "As gatekeepers to their days, our young students rely on us to be conscientious and informed facilitators of learning, willing to defend practices that match their unique stages of development."

Heidi works with educators to design learning experiences that respect their students' littleness. Still, the young learners in her charge have done things like build a model of their community and code a Bee-Bot to locate different favorite places; learn about each other's families; solve problems related to nurturing our earth; participate in a multitude of STEAM experiences; bravely perform a variety of storybook reenactments; and play in dramatic play centers designed to be caves, weather broadcast booths, construction zones, ice cream shops, and pumpkin patches—just to list a few. These same students also learned how to respect others, be a friend, regulate their emotions, and give their best efforts time and time again.

Heidi believes that early childhood education should be the start—not the end—of developmentally appropriate instruction. The choice, educators, is ours! May we never forget that every day has the potential to be magical for a child, and while our youngest learners are in early childhood programs, pledge with me to let them be little, for they will only be this precious age once.

That doesn't mean we stop taking their education seriously, though—or stop teaching them. All of our school staff at Woodson have a "high expectations, no excuses" mentality when it comes to the alignment of teaching toward essential outcomes in academic and social-emotional learning. Leading with this in mind, we schedule interventionists (math/reading, gifted and talent development, special education teachers, EL teachers, speech pathologists) into every PLC meeting. That way when we are talking about a student who is struggling, or a student who is exceeding, we have an intervention teacher on board and offering suggestions to support each learner. Even more vital is having the leader there as well. Attending leadership meetings and rotating through PLC meetings not only supports the teachers, but enhances your own understanding of the learning occurring in your school—and allows you to guide it to both high expectations and developmentally appropriate activities.

Creating a common foundation of learning targets across all school stakeholders is critical for developing those developmentally appropriate instructional opportunities. At Woodson, we took half a school year to dive deeper into the Minnesota State Standards. First, to understand vocabulary differentiation between K through third grade, then the concepts, and finally to give feedback as to what was missing from the standards, but key to success in the later grades, in our experience. After compiling this information, a team of educators and an outside expert locked themselves in the conference room for a day and hashed out the essential outcomes students needed to master before exiting kindergarten. Once the school had reviewed these, a different team pulled together to create common formative assessments for each outcome, as well as ways in which teams could monitor and celebrate student success on a weekly basis. Teachers passionate about technology bridged lessons that integrated Smart Board activities and Thinking Maps, to extend and deepen the concepts. All of this information was then posted to our shared Office 365 site so that all team members could have access to the work. Our instructional coach created a parent-friendly one-pager that explained the different concepts, how they would be measured, and how they could help their child at home.

By the end of the process, we had created a way to keep the learning fun while setting high expectations, track students and the way to best teach them, and make the transition into bringing the parents into the picture as well. It was the ideal example of taking our jobs seriously, but having fun with them—and making sure that our littlest learners were being set up for success.

Taking the time to assess where students are and where they need to go across grade levels is a time-consuming, taxing process. It is, however, necessary if you want to create a vision of high expectations with a target in mind. Wherever you decide to start, just do it. From your first common formative assessment to a full-blown PLC meeting with norms, essential outcomes, and feedback loops, this work is wide, and has many points to jump in at.

Wherever you start, make sure to celebrate the small successes along the way. Teaching is rewarding and fulfilling, but if you don't take time to stop and smell the roses, you risk losing the passion and purpose you came into the profession with—and the focus on making a difference for those you serve. Taking the time for a rest stop during the journey will prepare everyone for the work ahead, while allowing everyone to celebrate the steps thus far.

MORE HEART; LESS HAMMER

Incorporating social-emotional learning as a core curriculum

"Let's start at the very beginning."
—THE SOUND OF MUSIC

THE PROBLEM: SCHOOLS DON'T UNDERSTAND THEM; THEY JUST SUSPEND THEM

THE NEEDS OF students today continue to be more and more complex. What's more, the supports available to these learners can be highly individualized, and require teachers, leaders, and families to practice deeper patience and understanding. To identify deficits in learning, we must figure out what a child needs to know and do successfully, in order to be successful in school. As educators, we must all commit to supporting and holding all students to high expectations, with no excuses and no quitting.

One of the most disturbing trends I've seen while working in early education is the opposite of that. In fact, it's the tendency to suspend and even expel students ... from preschool. According to a report released by the Department of Education Office of Civil Rights (10/28/16):

- Black preschool children are 3.6 times more likely to receive one or more out-of-school suspensions as white preschool children.

- Black boys represent 19 percent of male preschool enrollment, but make up 45 percent of male preschool children receiving one or more out-of-school suspensions.

- Black girls represent 20 percent of female preschool enrollment, but make up 54 percent of female preschool children receiving one or more out-of-school suspensions.

- Most public preschool children suspended are boys. While boys represent 54 percent of preschool enrollment, they represent 78 percent of preschool children receiving one or more out-of-school suspensions.

The trend continues with our most high-need populations of students in our K–12 school system.

- Children with disabilities served by the Individuals with Disabilities Education Act (IDEA) represent 20 percent of preschool enrollment, but make up 15 percent of preschool children receiving one or more out-of-school suspensions.

- English learners represent 12 percent of pre-school enrollment, but make up 7 percent of pre-school children receiving one or more out-of-school suspensions.

This reactive response to behavior affects students emotionally, financially, and educationally. It also significantly impacts the outcomes of those students, teachers' abilities to reach students and establish a positive rapport, and school relationships with families.

What message is this sending to our youngest learners? You can come to our school *if* you are ready for our rules, our expectations, and our ways of learning. In that case, the idea of being ready for school needs to be clearly redefined. The adults serving our earliest and most vulnerable learners need to be ready for all students—not the other way around.

Learning how to approach them from a skill development level, rather than through a deficit model, will provide a more positive return than kicking children (and families) out of our schools.

THE HACK: MORE HEART; LESS HAMMER

Having a school culture that focuses on social-emotional learning allows everyone an opportunity to learn and relearn, and teach or reteach every day, with the goal of ensuring that all students have the supports necessary—socially and academically—to be successful in school.

One way to define social-emotional readiness is to find specific ways to help students:

- Form and positively engage in relationships with other students and adults.

- Practice empathy and develop an understanding of other people's feelings and how we impact and influence those feelings.

- Express and manage a full range of emotions in ways that are socially acceptable and fit school and community norms.

- Develop a lifelong love for learning.

Moreover, taking the time to define how to implement these key readiness skills will help a school implement social-emotional learning in all environments of the school with consistency.

So how do we go about doing it? Start by visualizing social-emotional learning as a stool with three legs: self-regulation, character development, and a framework for consistent implementation and ways to monitor student and adult success. In order for that stool to be solid, school leadership teams have to develop plans in *each* of these three areas. And they need to do so with more heart and less hammer—so that the students have the best chance for success.

Setting the ground rules for how school works. One of the first and most important things to think about when it comes to social-emotional learning is making students—and their parents—feel more comfortable about what they're getting into. Walking into a school for the first time can be a little overwhelming. This is, after all, a place full of hidden challenges for both students and parents. And a lot has changed since the parents themselves went to school.

Think about all that has changed since *you* were a student— and the nightmare scenarios parents might have heard about from others. Many students and parents might come into a situation worried that they'll find teachers who are too strict, and an inflexible program that doesn't take individual students into account.

Those are the things you need to start with. How are you going to demonstrate the *new* ways of going to school, for those who are coming into our classrooms for the very first time? How are you going to demonstrate that you believe in heart over hammer, and giving the students a better learning environment?

Creating a learning playbook that doesn't come from state standards or a textbook is essential to ensuring that all students are comfortable in any school environment. This playbook can be a framework for what the student and staff expectations are in each area of the school. It's a pattern, so that students know what's expected of them—and what they can expect of others. Find ideas and examples for generating these frameworks through the use of Positive Behavioral Systems and Supports (PBIS). At the elementary age, and especially with pre-K/K students, behavioral frameworks help to erase any "gray" areas of expectation, and give everyone a clear picture.

Here is an example. Go into your cafeteria on one of the first days of school, and observe the difference between K lunch and fifth-grade lunch. Notice a few things? The kindergarteners are probably being more difficult—but does that mean that they're going to be challenging cohorts? Do you need to give over 50 percent of them lunch detention because they still can't open their milk after practicing for three days? And goodness, what is wrong with the teachers? Four days in, these students might still clump together when leaving the lunchroom, while the older students form in nice lines. Starting to see the picture?

The kindergarteners don't know what to do yet. But does that mean you should react with discipline and a lecture? Should you use the hammer? Or should you try something gentler first?

One way to teach behavioral expectations with heart over hammer is to show students the school expectations in a natural environment, and in a way that shows students what it should look like. Videos, social stories, and practicing in the natural environment multiple times can help to set a successful stage for students. Even routines like using the bathroom are going to be new for children who have never been in a school environment before. If they came from an in-home daycare, or their parents cared for them until school age, using a bathroom with multiple other five-year-olds is going to be a new experience. And nevermind adding an automatic flushing system (as we did)! A handful of students every year suddenly became afraid to use that bathroom.

Instead of sending them home or disciplining them for misbehaving, we set up a system where we showed them it was okay, and started sending them to the bathroom with friends, until they were comfortable enough to go by themselves.

When it comes to character development, you'll find many programs out there that address students. Finding ones that meet the development needs for the age of your students is critical for its success. Tools such as the *What Works Clearinghouse* (www.ies. ed.gov/ncee/wwc) can help break down the different curriculums out there by grade level, skills developed, and evidence of effectiveness. Using developmentally appropriate tools is vital to success here—for both the staff and the students themselves.

Self-regulation is an area of social-emotional learning that is still growing in schools, especially in the area of young learners. Books like *Yardsticks* by Chip Wood help educators understand the development milestones children will be mastering at each age. Take the time to learn these milestones before you establish a set of tools for supporting students in their navigation of school experiences. Become proactive about helping students identify their own emotions, and regulate them. You will find this to be far more powerful than reactive punishments are, when their behavioral responses do not meet the hidden curriculum of rules of your school.

WHAT YOU CAN DO TOMORROW

- **Create a team.** As with any important work at a school, you need to start by creating a team to help you build a comprehensive plan for moving forward. Our school created a team that went on to develop a list of school expectations for every environment, and then put together lesson plans for teaching these skills in a consistent manner across the entire school. The leadership team is made up of teachers, specialists, a social worker, a behavior interventionist, and paraprofessionals, and also seeks feedback from students—who can also be a part of the team. They review school behavior data (tracked in our School-Wide Information System, or SWIS), take time to read and recognize staff member positive referral cards, offer monthly reflections at staff meetings, and problem-solve other issues that directly impact the climate of the school during the year. This team will be your go-to when it comes to making school-wide decisions about goals for students, and will make sure that your policy uses heart over hammer for social-emotional learning.

- **Look for the root cause.** Have conversations with a few teachers about behavioral concerns the teachers have noticed during the first few days of school. Work with the teachers to identify behavioral concerns to specific students, and then assign teachers the job of coming up with plans.

  You'll be amazed at what these simple first-day steps lead to. Review the plans the teacher develops with your team, but follow my advice, and check each student's cumulative file before you meet with their parents! When my team has checked those files, we've found that while we might have thought we were dealing with a defiant child who did not want to follow directions or work with others, the truth was that we were dealing with a child who had never gone to preschool. And wow, does that shift the conversation. All of a sudden, you're working with a child who had never experienced waiting in line, taking turns, or following the other routines associated with school experiences.

  At that point, it might be necessary to redo the plan, starting with developing initial school skills rather than distinguishing defiant behaviors. But start with the root cause of the issue, and be strategic with your intention. At home, if my son starts sneezing, I have two choices: Is it allergies or a cold? The treatments are different, and if I don't know the cause, the treatment will take longer.

  As educators, finding the real reason so you

can treat the problem correctly is worth the work. And this will start—in your first-day exercises—with identifying any students who are having issues.

- **Find ways to deepen everyone's learning.** Social-emotional learning is not just about the students. The adults in the school also need opportunities to enhance, develop, and implement strategies that will deepen their own understanding of the needs of students, and the supports the teachers can provide. Start a list of ways to help your teachers grow and branch out in this manner.

  One way our school has approached this learning is through book clubs. As a staff, we choose books that might represent a need we have, a population of students we serve, or a new intervention that we are interested in implementing. Our books have ranged from topics about disabilities, students coming from other countries, emotional/behavioral disorders, and family engagement. Each study offers questions and, if possible, speakers on the topic at hand.

  Recognizing that the adults in the building need professional development and then providing it regularly will help your school see the need for resources, and then treat them. Go to Facebook, Twitter, and your personal network to start sketching out ideas for satisfying that particular need.

- **Practice what we teach.** Start figuring out how to use the systems you have for students on the staff as well. One way we learn together is by implementing the student tools with the staff. We have Staff Recognition Cards that are written for specific reasons and can be given by anyone—just like our student recognition cards. Staff have their own check-in chip for our self-regulation curriculum, including the office staff. We also take time during the year to fill out behavior referrals on case studies as a school staff, to check for consistencies in reporting and determine whether any clarifications are needed in documentation processes. Modeling the tools we want our students to use means we have a better understanding of how these will be received—and gives us an opportunity to learn for ourselves. Write down some things that your school staff can start using in this regard, for better learning and development of your teachers.

A BLUEPRINT FOR FULL IMPLEMENTATION

Step 1: Invest early.

"It is never too early, but it is also never too late." This is a mantra I have heard Steve Tozer, Ph.D., Professor in Educational Policy Studies at the University of Illinois at Chicago, and Founding Director of the UIC Center for Urban Education Leadership, say many times—and it definitely aligns with the work of creating successful environments for all students!

Start early, and be consistent. What supports can you think about getting ready for students in the spring, before they arrive in the fall? Ask local preschools to provide multiple opportunities to visit their settings, for teachers to meet their future classes. Observing pre-K students in their natural setting can give you ideas on how to structure for success as the students transition to kindergarten. What are the pre-K classes doing, and how can you transition that to your own class? Involve other team members, too, such as your school social worker, school psychologist, and special education teachers, and hold transition meetings in the spring to meet with pre-K special education staff. Ask them specific questions about what environmental supports have benefited the students. The more you know, the better you can serve the students you will have tomorrow.

Step 2: Don't forget about Tier 1.

So many times, we rush to ensure that our core academic supports are in place and gloss over critical components of social-emotional learning structures. At our school, we have invested a framework for identifying and teaching behavioral expectations in all school domains, to create a positive school environment for all stakeholders—and to make sure that teaching isn't forgotten. This framework is aligned with the work of Positive Behavioral Interventions and Supports. While we dedicate time specifically to teaching these skills during the first ten days of school, our PBIS leadership team reviews results throughout the year, to determine whether reteaching needs to occur. As leaders, we have to make sure the adults are supporting the students in meeting academic and social targets. For example, use the 80 percent rule as a guide—if more than 20 percent of our student population is struggling with recess time, it means there's a system issue. And in that case, the adults need to fix it—rather than punishing the students.

Take the time to build a framework or plan in your school, to make sure your teachers—and your students—are staying on track in their progress.

Step 3: Put together a plan for making decisions.

If you have students not responding to core social-emotional behavioral supports, treat it as you would a student who has academic struggles. Students who move into our Tier 2 level of behavioral interventions are reviewed by our RtI team, which works to determine the function of the behavior—and then provide appropriate interventions to meet that student's specific needs. After implementing core instruction in social-emotional learning, our school offers tiered supports that work to solve specific problem behaviors. The school RtI team meets to review students who are struggling with core instruction, looks over our behavioral data (we use SWIS), and makes recommendations regarding interventions for the student. These might range from social stories to informal check-ins, sticker charts for specific behaviors, or entrance into our check-in/check-out program. No matter the intervention, data is collected and reviewed every four to six weeks to determine effectiveness of our plans, and make changes when necessary.

Work with your school to put together a system that works for you. Treating the misbehavior as an opportunity to find new ways to reach the child will help maintain your school-wide expectations, and help the individual students as well.

Step 4: Involve parents every step of the way.

In the early grades, parents need to be completely aware of concerns, and participate in problem-solving. They were not only their child's first teacher, but their primary teacher until entering school, and have the best view of any child's unique needs. But put together a specific process for knowing when to get in touch with parents. At our school, if a student is reported for three major behavioral referrals, it triggers the RtI team to start studying the case. When that happens, the classroom teacher fills out paperwork, including putting together a brief parent questionnaire. Questions range from birth to present and include information on developmental milestones (crawling, walking, talking), previous school experiences, and any home concerns. Occasionally, I am able to do the parent interview, and appreciate the opportunity to have a one-on-one conversation about strengths, challenges, and ways that they have worked through issues with their children. Taking the time to ask questions and establish a working relationship with parents early on helps to establish a long-term plan that is supported by all team members.

Step 5: Love them first, then help them learn.

When I moved from middle school to kindergarten, the first few students who visited my office really opened up my eyes to behavioral intent. The function of behavior in middle school is very different than the function in kindergarten—even if the behavioral incident is almost identical. For example, "fights" on the playground. In the five years I have been leading and learning with kindergarteners, I've found that the main function of fighting on the playground has been a lack of skills for communicating with peers. So punishment—especially out of context—has not changed the behavior. However, heading back out to the playground with the "offender" and "victim" and talking through the scenario has almost always solved the problem.

Likewise, a student who is having a hard time sitting still in class is not always trying to disrupt the lesson—but might need a bathroom break, and be too afraid to ask.

Identify the core function of behaviors in kindergarteners, and then work with a team to support the learner and provide a child with a more educational opportunity, rather than punishment. *Love them first, then help them learn.*

Step 6: Take a pause.

In recent years, we had five students with significant behavior issues that had teachers, parents, support staff, and myself pulling out our hair. None of the tools we had used in the past were working with this group, and we all started to have heavy hearts because we were reacting to their behavior rather than responding to core needs. After a particularly difficult week, we pulled our RtI team together to review our processes. And suddenly we realized that we didn't have a tool for this situation. We were lacking a flow chart for responses to behavior, and a menu of options. By taking the time to pause, regroup, and brainstorm, we came up with at least five ways to redirect the particular student in class; five ways to redirect, regroup, and return a student to class from a break space; and five ways to regroup and return to class from the office. This template gave us consistent tools besides ISS or OSS (in-school suspension; out-of-school suspension) for our young learners, and empowered the adults on the team in regard to choosing a tool that worked in a specific situation.

But it never would have worked if we hadn't taken a step back and let ourselves breathe. Include this step back on your list of possible tools (see example below in Image 4.1), for when nothing else seems to be working.

Response to Challenging Behavior Template
Student Name:
Team Members Involved:
Target Behavior: *Stay safe in school by staying in class and not running in building or out of school.*

Level 1: In Class Response	Level 2: Take A Break Response	Level 3: Office Response
i. Student Desk—individualized space to work if refusal to complete group tasks.	i. 5 Minute Timed Break	i. Desk in Office with sensory tools available.
ii. Modify work	ii. Visual Processing Sheet	ii. Set 10 minute timer for regulation time (do not talk about problem at this time).
iii. Zones of Regulation board (Kaplan)	iii. Visual Schedule of tasks to complete and timer for return to class.	iii. Use visual processing worksheet for student to use to communicate.
iv. 1:1 positive feedback from teacher/para/special education teacher/para	iv. Classroom teacher/Behavior Interventionist switch spaces so teacher can maintain relationship with child.	iv. Offer child the opportunity to call parent with staff and explain what happened and what we will do differently to regroup and return to class.
v. Motivator to have more consistent response to desired behavior.	v. Break area close to classroom (conference room?)	v. If #2 is not successful allow child to complete the tasks they missed in office for an extended break and then try #3 again.

Image 4.1

85

Step 7: Relationships, Relationships, Relationships.

Jimmy Casas (@Casas_Jimmy), author, former high school principal, and current national speaker, lives by the three R's and their importance in what educators do on a daily basis. Unless every child in your school can identify one adult who cares unconditionally, you are failing every child in your school. I have observed the most masterful teachers build such incredible bonds with students that even ten years later, those children, now sophomores in high school, remember specific situations with the teacher.

If you or a teacher are struggling in building those relationships, find others who can model, guide, and offer suggestions on how to find the greatness in each child. Meet with the parents, guardians, child care providers, or previous teachers to find out what worked, and how you can build on it.

As we said earlier, it is never too early, and never too late—and is it never acceptable to give up on a five-year-old.

OVERCOMING PUSHBACK

If I do it this way, skill development will be deficient. In Ross Greene's book, *Lost and Found*, the author covers a mantra that my staff uses when pushing the importance of social-emotional learning in schools: Kids do well if they can.

 Operating through the ups and downs with a mindset of "what can I teach" versus "what the child can't learn" shifts the focus from a problem to a skill development mentality.

A lot of the time, educators (and leaders) unintentionally assume that students walk into school already holding the appropriate behaviors needed to be successful. But often, these students actually walk in the front door with *no* understanding of the hidden curriculum that will determine whether they are labeled as good or bad. I think back to my son's first few days in preschool, when he entered a class of eighteen other students who had been in school since September. He started in January, with only two weeks of life experience in America. Coming from an orphanage, his core control was weak, so sitting criss-cross applesauce was physically difficult for him. Limited exposure to the English language also meant that for much of those first months, he was lost, and trauma exposure meant that anytime anyone brushed against him or attempted to touch him, his anxiety and stress went through the roof—and manifested itself by him running out of rooms, or retaliating physically toward others.

We have all had that child in our classrooms or schools, but how we provided support and services runs the gamut. It's not a question of providing love and failing to teach them the skills they need. But understanding the intention of the behavior—and finding ways to support the student while continuing to have high expectations—is a delicate process. Supports that worked one day, might not work the next. You may have three great weeks and then suddenly be back to square one. Operating through the ups and downs with a mindset of "what can I teach" versus "what the child can't learn" shifts the focus from a problem to a skill development mentality.

But sometimes retention is the only choice. Kindergarten retention can be a very sensitive subject—for all team members. Teachers want to make sure students are socially and academically ready for the rigor of the next grade, parents want their child to be successful, and leaders want to see all students excited and engaged in their learning. I have heard of school sites retaining students on the basis of a gut feeling, attendance, or even students not knowing all their letter sounds. In talking with parents, I know that this can sometimes come as a complete surprise to them—something that wasn't discussed or decided on until the last moment.

When I was leading at the secondary level, I thought going through the expulsion process was the most difficult thing I would ever do— until I had my first kindergarten retention conference. Making decisions about having a child repeat a grade should be done with a spelled-out process, and in a way that is recognized by the school district and decided by a full school team. These decisions should never be made in a one-and-done conversation. Teachers should be communicating with the principal as soon as October if they have concerns about students, and leaders should be sitting in on those conferences, building solid relationships with families, well before May.

One area that impacts early learning significantly is school attendance. But waiting until the end of the year and retaining a student (and their family) because of school attendance is a very reactive solution that doesn't solve the problem. In fact, it only causes further frustration for all team members.

To support the two perspectives in this conversation, I work with families during the fall, to discuss the critical importance of school attendance and the impact on learning when a child misses or is late to school multiple times a week. I work with previous schools and through preschool transition meetings to figure out which students had difficulties coming to school or getting to school on time, and then monitor attendance right away in kindergarten. Teachers team up with me to offer tools that families can access at home, to fill any gaps that have opened up due to the attendance concerns. This allows families to have a greater understanding of not only the importance of school attendance, but also their role in ensuring their children are in school, to help them continue to learn.

Instead of reacting immediately with retention, use your process to plan ahead to address these problems beforehand, and lead the students to greater success.

But do the parents really have to be involved? Before making assumptions and creating detailed plans focusing on the student behavior, ask the team whether anyone has talked with the family. Including families as soon as problems arise creates a sense of trust, understanding, and partnership in this work, rather than a sense of fault or blame. Including them in the problem-solving process might also shed light on concerns teachers are seeing in school. As part of our student assistance team, we ask teachers to meet with parents so they can fill out a questionnaire that looks at developmental milestones, previous school experiences, and other factors that could be impacting the student's learning. Meeting with the parents and asking the right questions means you have an opportunity to get information and make the greatest impact on the situation.

Take Ross Greene's quote and change it to reflect on engaging families: *Parents do well if they can.* If parents ask for help, listen and work with them to find solutions. There's a chance that whatever you are seeing at school, they are seeing at home as well. Find out what works, and what happens, so you can start right away on solutions. Make copies of visual schedules, create a school/home notebook, and offer to come to the home and observe the behavior firsthand, to build the relationship with the family. Support parents through challenging situations at school and home, because if we want their child to succeed, we need their help as well.

THE HACK IN ACTION

When establishing a core social-emotional curriculum in your school, you must understand that you teach the whole child, not just the parts that fit into your perceived "model student" box. No one student comes into the education setting with the same experiences as another. Therefore, there is no one right way to offer social-emotional learning for all students.

When Katy Phinney (@KatyPhinney), a pre-K program specialist at Richardson ISD in Texas, first began teaching pre-K thirteen years ago, she knew it was important to teach children how to problem-solve, but her social-emotional teacher toolbox was empty. Through her school experiences, she quickly learned that social-emotional learning is the answer to practically everything. She has found that when we focus on teaching the whole child, it sets the foundation for future success in all areas of life. Children feel empowered to tackle whatever lies ahead, know how to self-regulate their emotions, and build meaningful and respectful relationships with their peers and adults. All of these things must be modeled and taught, and a large portion of that learning happens in the classroom. And the bonus is having a family structure that supports healthy social-emotional learning at home.

In 2011, her school district adopted the Frog Street Pre-K curriculum, which includes a Conscious Discipline module as part of the morning routine and positive classroom environment. This is when Katy threw the color-changing clip chart in the trash. Conscious Discipline helped her understand that the adults must have positive intentions for children, be able to remain calm, and model healthy problem-solving strategies. Then we can teach the children to do the same!

At Woodson, we developed a matrix of behaviors for every school environment (see Image 4.2 below), and videos of students demonstrating these behaviors. Social stories and lesson plans are delivered not only at the start of the school year, but as boosters during the course of the school year. Throughout the year, we collect data to determine whether the initial lessons were effective, need to be reviewed, or require some changes to meet the needs of students.

	CARING CRITTERS TAKE CARE OF THEMSELVES.	CARING CRITTERS TAKE CARE OF OTHERS.	CARING CRITTERS TAKE CARE OF PROPERTY.
Classroom	Use inside voice 1, 2, 3 Listen and follow staff directions Try your best	Hands and feet to self Follow staff directions Listen, be caring and polite	Use furniture and materials appropriately Keep classroom clean
Lunchroom	Use inside voice 1, 2, 3 Eat your food Stay seated Raise your hand for help	Hands and feet to self Use good manners	Two hands on tray Dump and stack tray appropriately Keep your space clean
Hallway	Use silent voice – 1 Eyes forward Walking feet	Set a good example Hands and feet to self Follow staff directions	Hands and feet to self Keep hallway clean
Bathroom	Use whisper voice 1 or 2 Go to bathroom Flush Wash your hands	Respect others privacy Set a good example	Keep area clean Report empty supplies
Play Centers	Use inside voice 1, 2, 3 Use walking feet	Be kind to others Take turns Share Include others Give a helping hand Play safely Gentle touch Use equipment appropriately Tell an adult if someone is hurt	Use and clean up materials appropriately Report missing and broken materials
Boost Up	Use inside voice 1, 2, 3 Use body control Follow directions of staff	Hands and feet to self Take turns	Use and clean up materials appropriately Report missing and broken materials
Playground	Use outside voice 1, 2, 3, 4 Line up when bell rings Follow staff directions Use equipment appropriately	Be kind to others Share Include others Give a helping hand Play safely Gentle touch Use equipment Tell an adult if someone is hurt	Backpack on Critter Line Use and clean up toys appropriately Take care of nature
Bus	Use inside voice 1, 2, 3 Stay out of the Danger Zone Stay seated	Hands and feet to self Be kind to others Follow driver directions	Keep bus clean

Image 4.2

Embedded into our social studies curriculum units are character themes and traits. Teachers have access to a core curriculum around each trait, but are encouraged to enhance and provide learning experiences to match the needs of the individual students in their classrooms. At the end of each month, the school social worker and myself role-play, read a story, or reenact demonstrations of the character traits. And at the end of each assembly, the classroom teachers come up and recognize the student of the month in their classes—the ones who did their very best to exemplify the skill.

Five years into this work, we realized we were missing a link to this learning. Students knew the expectations for each area of the school, and understood the different character traits, like persistence, caring, gratitude, and respect. However, when it came to them applying these skills in support of their own self-regulation throughout the day, we realized we hadn't found the right supports quite yet.

After a year of learning, we eliminated classroom behavior clip charts, names on the board, and other reactive ways of identifying students who were struggling with self-regulation. And with the help of a grant from the Minnesota Department of Education, we invited Leah Kuypers, creator of the Zones of Regulation, to train our entire school staff on implementing the Zones for students during the following school year.

Now, the school's daily schedule offers formal and informal opportunities to provide direct instruction on social-emotional learning throughout the day. Daily morning greetings and self-regulation check-ins, embedded time during our social studies blocks to study various character traits, and modeling from students and staff in our play centers and boost-up areas are just a few of the ways we have implemented this.

The monthly character themes are published in our curriculum map, and we review key components in our PLC meetings, as well as within our RtI team. Each year, one of our site goals always includes a social-emotional component, and is tied to a measurement system. During every staff meeting, the first fifteen minutes are time to reflect, model gratitude, share celebrations, and provide resources around PBIS and social-emotional learning for all.

We have also implemented multiple data sources to monitor core instruction, as well as individual student needs. SWIS (School-Wide Information System) is our student behavior stool for monitoring behavior, and more specifically, the time of day, day of the week, and function of the behavior. We also have a behavior screener for all students in the fall, and then as needed through the year for students who are lacking necessary school readiness skills—and whose behavior is becoming a barrier to their learning.

All of this is communicated to families during the course of the year. Explaining what we are trying to teach, why it is important, and how they can help support at home shows families that we truly need their help for the success of their child at school—and home.

What gets monitored gets done, right? If you truly want to ensure that all students are leaving your school with the necessary social-emotional outcomes to be successful in school and life, you need to be accountable for the time, spaces, and ways for accomplishing this work.

For too long, I focused too much on academic learning over the social-emotional needs of students. Further into this journey, I have found there is a balance between the two worlds, and that one will not be successful without the other. Self-regulation, understanding classroom expectations, and understanding the feelings of others are critical components to the learning of our future leaders.

What I learned from working with middle school students still holds true in early learning: Fear doesn't change behavior, but positive, trusting relationships can. Having a school culture that gives social-emotional learning a growth mindset allows everyone an opportunity to learn, relearn, teach, or reteach every day, with the goal of making sure all students have the supports—socially and academically—to be successful in school.

FIND YOUR TECHNOLOGY FOCUS

Adding creativity, computational thinking, and coding

"The power of technology lies in its ability to ignite creativity and bring people together."
—BRAD GUSTAFSON, *RENEGADE LEADERSHIP*

THE PROBLEM: TECHNOLOGY IS SEEN AS NO MORE THAN A TOY

WANT TO START a heated conversation between parents and educators? Just bring up the use of technology with young children. IPads, cell phones, tablets, gaming devices, laptops … the list goes on and on. Both students and adults are in an age where the daily percentage of time spent on devices of some sort might be higher than the percentage of time spent interacting with others, and it's necessary to talk about that from an educational standpoint.

The key to this conversation, though, it to avoid making it an all-or-nothing issue. Instead, find ways to use technology to enhance learning. This conversation also can't be had in isolation. Talk to leaders and educators from pre-K through 12th grade to help brainstorm foundational skills using technology—things that can be built today that will enhance learning tomorrow.

Innovation, technology, and creativity are buzz words across the field of education—and have become the big, shiny new thing in teaching. As an educator or a school leader, it is hard *not* to jump in with both feet, considering the incredible new technologies for education. However, laying a solid, firm, and intentional foundation is key to ensuring that you will have the stamina to keep up with the goals you set in September.

THE HACK: FIND YOUR TECHNOLOGY FOCUS

Curious about how to incorporate technology into your schools and classrooms? Before you start, make sure you can answer this question: What are your goals for implementing technology? Because if you're going to do this successfully—and intentionally— to create opportunities for authentic student voice and learning, you need to have a plan in place before you start. Start with a few simple concepts.

What is your vision? Before you start, do you know where you want to end? For example, when we started the #PackInTrain coding club, our focus was to expose students to the foundational vocabulary of coding and computational thinking, while demonstrating how we might use technology in the early grades. Think about the intentional connections in your school. Could iPads in classrooms provide opportunities for students to practice concepts key to outcomes and standards? Smart Boards or other interactive systems can be used by students to manipulate, create, or design learning in the moment. And teachers can use the same tools to create boards for their students to use independently.

Don't be afraid to try. Leading with innovation means you might not have all the answers before you start. You might also end up trying something that you don't necessarily know how to use. Start small by signing up for a code.org session or logging into scratchjr. org, and trying it out without a finished product in mind. Pilot test some sort of technology into your school to see how the teachers use it, what could be enhanced, and what you didn't think about when you started. By reflecting this way, you might end up finding additional uses and intentional ways to amplify student voice and learning.

Ask for help. In this work, isolation can be the number one enemy. Thinking you can do it all by yourself limits opportunities to enhance what has already been done. On the other hand, asking other teachers to come in and observe a classroom that's using some sort of tech is a great way to gain feedback, while demonstrating the growth mindsets you want your teachers and students to have when learning. Showing that level of vulnerability can also build trust within the school team, and bring about key insights into making the learning even better.

Regardless of the technology or tool used, make sure you can draw a direct line to student learning, strategic plans, and opportunities to offer creative and innovative learning experiences for all students. This will help you avoid the "technology is just for play" label, and focus on innovative learning instead.

WHAT YOU CAN DO TOMORROW

- **Find their passion and make a path.** Sometimes, we get so caught up in what everyone else is doing that we forget to ask those who are directly impacted by our decisions—our students. When you are implementing technology, are you asking students how this is helping them learn? Are you asking them what could help learning in their school/classroom be even better? Utilizing the voice of your school community is critical to ensuring that you are doing the right things for the right reasons. Tomorrow, seek out students and parents, and ask them their opinions on what's exciting and motivating for your students at home. It won't always be the same thing that schools are doing. As educators, we need to equip ourselves and our colleagues with the skills to ensure that all our learners are reaching their highest levels. This might mean reading a book, following a blog, attending a conference, or visiting other schools that are implementing this incredibly important work. Start collecting student ideas and choices in this regard, to make your classes and school more engaging, relevant, and creative with technology.

- **Start small and go from there.** As adults, we are learning how to learn differently than we did as students, and you have to give yourself grace in that experience. Don't expect to know it all right from the beginning. Instead, start with one question or goal, and go from there. For example, a coding club could be a vehicle to enhancing computational thinking, and something that would benefit students throughout the K–12 school experience. Come up with one coding activity as a whole group and move it to a learning station; have a makerspace day on an early release day; or, if you are the principal, seek out a few students and play a coding game or introduce them to a robot, iPad app, or other tool. As you go, see where they take the learning. It will probably not be where you thought you would direct them—but it will give you a clue about where to start in the future.

- **Ask others.** Intentionally integrating technology is critical to getting it right from the start. The investment of time, resources, and tools can be expensive, so you want to make sure you are making the right decisions the first time. Connect with others via hashtags on Twitter to ask questions and get a feel for what others are doing, and don't be afraid to connect with others with questions about books on integrating technology. Find your PLN and use them. The value they add will have a direct implication for the students you serve.

A BLUEPRINT FOR FULL IMPLEMENTATION

Step 1: Find a framework.

Before you start, find out where your district wants all students to go. District leadership and technology integrationists in our district created Essential Technology Outcomes, which are broken down by grade level and bands such as Device Usage, Tools and Application, Citizenship and Literacy, and Innovative Practices. This framework guides implementation of device usage, and also lays out the learning objectives from K through 12th grade. If you are looking for a place to start in regard to creating your own outcomes, ISTE (International Society for Technology in Education) and Future Ready Schools have also developed frameworks that will guide your work.

Step 2: Listen to the learners—all of them.

Today's educators are being asked to incorporate tools that were not even imaginable when they were in school. For a lot of us, this means that finding ways to embed these new tools into today's classrooms brings with it a healthy helping of fear and concern! What if the students break something? What if they don't know what to do—and I don't either? How will I fix something if it breaks? Allow the educators time to share their concerns and questions up front, to give them a chance to build a foundation of knowledge and applications first. By listening to their questions, you'll develop a deeper understanding of the way in which you should create a program—and a path that addresses the needs of both students and teachers. Tying in content vocabulary from the classroom, and mirroring learning objectives from PLC discussions, allows for a more seamless connection between learning and the technology programs you're building—for both teachers and students!

Step 3: Reflect, review, and revise.

Pioneering this work in the early years means you're laying out the first pathways for students. Moving forward, you might become the lead pioneer in your school, district, county, or maybe even your state. So you want to make sure that you're doing something that *works*. Try something, reflect on how it went, review the steps you took, and revise the plan for tomorrow. Having something on paper and then putting it into play with a class of students between three and eight years of age is a dynamic opportunity. Take down student responses and then tailor instructions to meet their needs before you try again. When done well, the tools, the students, and the learning will reach levels you never dreamed.

OVERCOMING PUSHBACK

They can't do that! When researching coding clubs for kindergarten, I had a hard time finding other schools doing the work. Articles, blogs, and books had detailed lessons for intermediate and upper grades, but limited work in the primary grades. And the problem is this: A lot of times, educators and leaders who aren't deep in the work of early learning will make assumptions about what our students can or can't do, based upon preconceived notions of their own.

As in other aspects of early learning, we must not only lead and inspire our students, but advocate on their behalf about what they can do—even when adults think they can't. Commit to finding opportunities to connect with other leaders who are incorporating digital learning in their schools. The more you learn, read, and research, the more ways you will find to incorporate pre-coding and coding experiences that put students in the driver's seat of their learning. Integrating technology is no longer just "nice," but a necessity for early learners, and as adults, we have to get past our understanding of technology as a babysitting toy and recognize it as the tool and vehicle for learning it really can be.

They're just shiny new toys. Look, I will be the first to admit it: I like shiny new things. In my personal life, I am a sucker for end caps at the grocery store, and ads on Facebook can sidetrack me from my sweep of social media for the day. In my professional life, I can get multiple emails every day for a new curriculum, another speaker, or a new tech tool on the market—and each one is irresistible. Professional conferences can be overwhelming, due to the number of ideas and things you can take back tomorrow to your school.

Reframe the conversation from the amount of time spent on a device to what is occurring with the technology. Are students passively watching a video on an iPad, or logged into MIT's ScratchJr and programming a response to a prompted question from text?

At the same time, Twitter and Facebook can make educators depressed with all the things they are *not* doing to recognize staff, host parent meetings, or create that perfect bulletin board for back to school. This also holds true with the intentional integration of technology in schools—it's not always going to go exactly the way you think it will. And everything has to be judged based on your unique situation. Just because the school down the street just handed every five-year-old an iPad, doesn't necessarily mean it is the right thing for your students or your school. It is easy to get sucked into the newest thing, only to be discouraged when the implementation fails or the buy-in isn't as great as you thought it would be.

So instead of being distracted by the shiny new toys, make sure that whatever you choose aligns with the bigger picture for your school. It's critical to the success of the implementation—and the stress levels for you and your staff.

Too much technology; too young an age. Parents, educators, and other stakeholders will approach me in regard to the amount of time students are spending on devices and if there is really a need for technology in the early grades. While I firmly agree that a committed, dedicated, and high-quality teacher wins over technology every time, there can be a balance between the two. Reframe the conversation from the amount of time spent on a device to what is occurring with the technology. Are students passively watching a video on an iPad, or logged into MIT's ScratchJr and programming a response to a prompted question from text? Does the teacher have a video up of counting backward from twenty on YouTube, or are students working together to program a Bee-Bot robot to move along a path, finding numbers twenty-two through sixteen in backward order? Changing this conversation from how much to what is being done focuses on the work that we want to be happening.

THE HACK IN ACTION

The intersecting lines of parenting and principaling took a unique twist for me when my oldest son joined a robotics team. During the season, my Friday nights and weekends were spent watching a group of fifth- and sixth-graders create a robot from scratch and program it to complete tasks. The perseverance and passion these students had for this project was astounding to me, and the amount of time the kids spent out of class, preparing for the next session, was intriguing. It also made me think: *If they are doing this in fifth grade, why not K?*

My first step in creating a coding club was to review any current research and programming ideas being used. NAEYC (National Association for the Education of Young Children), Twitter, and connecting with other elementary principals gave me a foundation to start the journey. Mid-year, I was able to allocate a small amount of funds to purchase a locked cart, Bee-Bots, Spheros, and Osmo systems, and repurposed some old iPads to add to the coding club collection. The next step was offering professional development for the teachers to gain their perspective on what tools would be engaging for the students, and what learning they thought would best be amplified. Then they choose two students per class to participate.

I created weekly lesson plans and loaded them onto our school blog, and posted updates for families on Twitter (using #PackInTrain to track it), and with our Remind app. Students had journals and other opportunities to reflect on what they learned and how it helped them understand other kindergarten concepts.

This group started small … but it grows every year. Last year, coding club offered six full six-week sessions, and was co-taught by the district tech integrationist, who was a former high school mathematics teacher. His direct experience with the concepts students would need most in the ten years of school reaffirmed the direction and importance of the club.

Three years later, we have a .5 innovation coach who will be scaling the coding club, so *all* the students in our school have the opportunity that a few had before. By linking and aligning work, we made connections with learning, and were able to allocate FTE to scale the programming up and include the entire school—to the benefit of everyone.

Technology at any age can be a vehicle for enhanced connections and deeper learning—or a frustrating fork in the road. Ensuring that you are using technology to amplify or enhance learning already in place allows for clear purpose and alignment to learning outcomes. It is easy to teach to the tool; the challenge is integrating the tool to the teaching.

Make sure that all staff have a foundational understanding of the role of technology, and advocate for professional development to ensure growth for the adults as well. They can only integrate it if they understand it! Reflecting on my own journey, the advice I would give anyone interested in starting this work would be: "What is the one thing I will do this year to amplify and innovate learning?"

The next step is learning to do it well.

PLEASE PUT PLAY BACK IN THE SCHOOL DAY

Innovating, aligning, and providing time for play and learning

"Play is the highest form of research."
—ALBERT EINSTEIN

THE PROBLEM: PLAY IS ESSENTIAL LEARNING, NOT AN EXTRA IN THE SCHOOL DAY

IF YOU ENGAGE in a conversation with teachers who have been teaching the younger years for the majority of their teaching career, you will hear the frustration of kindergarten becoming the new first grade. Tinkertoys, dress-up clothes, sand tables, and blocks have been packed up and put away. And with those boxes, students are losing the critical tools and time to develop academic skills with their peers in a natural—and fun—setting.

If you haven't taken time to look fully at the critical components of play in the school day, this is your wake-up call. Playful learning is fun, motivating, engaging, and creative. Play-based learning experiences can be accomplished without prerequisite academic skills, and can be executed in a manner that supports linguistically diverse students. Setting the stage for successful and intentional play-centered learning is certainly not easy. Done well, though, it is an orchestrated machine of students talking, sharing, working together, and using knowledge from the classroom to make connections to real-life applications. Resources such as the National Association for the Education of Young Children have many books, articles, and ideas on how to effectively integrate play back into the school day. Check out resources by early learning experts such as Rae Pica, as well. Rae is an incredible early learning leader who regularly shares her insights and ideas on play through her BAM Radio show, *Studentcentricity*, and through her YouTube channel, blog, and books.

In *Creative Schools*, Sir Ken Robinson, Ph.D., states, "Young children have a ready appetite to explore whatever draws their interests. When their curiosity is engaged, they will learn for themselves, from each other, and from any source they can lay their hands on." Taking that advice, why wouldn't you offer dedicated time, every day, to let their imaginations stretch and grow?

THE HACK: PLEASE PUT PLAY BACK IN THE SCHOOL DAY

Entering the world of play in the early grades requires your time, attention, and a willingness to see interactions differently—and more deeply. Observing children playing without knowing what they are doing and why they are doing it will actually keep you from investing in and advocating for play—because you don't understand it. Doing the deep work and understanding, on the other hand, will show you exactly why it's so important. So how do you go about doing this deep research?

Listen. One of the key indicators of a successful play-based lesson isn't in the actual lesson—it is in the preparation for the learning. Discuss with the teacher ahead of time what is going to happen during the lesson, to gain an understanding of the questions and routines that make the space and time successful for all students.

Learn. Reading multiple articles and books about the importance of play-based learning experiences for pre-K, K, and older grades (think makerspace, genius hour, and project based learning) is critical. In your research, you may learn that these spaces have different names but common themes: toys (or tools) of high interest; faces of dolls and things on the wall that represent the students in the class; and pre-teaching of social skills in the areas of communication, turn-taking, and questioning. These teachers have mastered the art of high-quality, higher-order thinking in a natural environment.

Play-based learning space can also be much more than free play. When done intentionally, this time becomes a natural environment where educators can weave academic concepts from the traditional classroom into fun games and projects. This time also allows students to engage in areas of interest in order to gain a deeper understanding of the application of the content.

Lead. After taking the time to learn about the science behind play centers, you'll be able to see how important this daily opportunity is for young learners. And that, in turn, will help you advocate for funds, and dedicate space and resources, to enhancing this learning space in schools. Lead your school through this by including stakeholders in this decision. Where does play fit in? Give tours to families, legislators, or other school leaders to show them your play space and advocate for this type of learning to occur daily in the early grades.

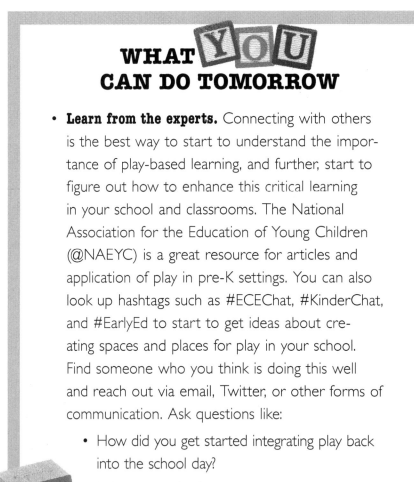

WHAT YOU CAN DO TOMORROW

- **Learn from the experts.** Connecting with others is the best way to start to understand the importance of play-based learning, and further, start to figure out how to enhance this critical learning in your school and classrooms. The National Association for the Education of Young Children (@NAEYC) is a great resource for articles and application of play in pre-K settings. You can also look up hashtags such as #ECEChat, #KinderChat, and #EarlyEd to start to get ideas about creating spaces and places for play in your school. Find someone who you think is doing this well and reach out via email, Twitter, or other forms of communication. Ask questions like:
  - How did you get started integrating play back into the school day?
  - When is this implemented during the day, and how do you incorporate learning targets?

- What is one thing you wish you would have thought of before you started?

- How do you share this learning with other teachers, leaders, and parents?

- How do you incorporate student voice and choice into decision-making?

- What tools (i.e., toys) have you found critical to enhancing play in your classroom?

Having an idea of what you are looking for and asking questions around your specific needs will help you bridge the gaps in your knowledge, with help from people already doing the work.

- **Schedule it into the day.** In our school, we have two dedicated classroom spaces for play centers that every class uses every day. We also have a committee that is dedicated to designing the space and activities to match monthly themes in the building. At the end of the month, the committees go into the play centers and rotate out stations, inventory current tools, and make recommendations for new materials or new ideas for the space. We also have professional development scheduled during the year and taught in the play centers, to enhance our knowledge and application of play-based instructional strategies. Topics about play have included the research behind why it is important, the cultural connections play has with the students we serve, and the incorporation of Bloom's taxonomy and higher-order thinking and questioning when structuring play activities.

Placing this time on our school schedule sends a message that playtime is as important as academic modules during the course of the day. Allocated professional development time to deepen our understanding and application of play also ensures that we continue to learn about enhancing the learning of our students.

Take some time tomorrow to figure out where playtime might go on your school's calendar—and how to make it happen.

- **Align it with established learning.**
  Prioritizing the importance of play-based learning also means incorporating funding and aligning it with your curriculum. When integrating play, we look at the academic and social outcomes for the month to find common themes. We draw from those to create ways we can weave the ideas into playful learning to reach learning targets.

  For example, our engineering unit brings out the creativity in both students and teachers in the play centers. In October, students have time to explore the various gourds and pumpkins the staff has brought for the sensory tables in our play centers. In November, they're given the opportunity to use a wide variety of tools to find the best way to move an object down a ramp without it falling off the track or going too quickly. I love watching students create towers with Magna-Tiles, make hypotheses with the sink-or-float activities, or use dramatic play items to recreate stories they've been telling in class.

Social-emotional concepts such as persistence, self-regulation, and collaboration are pre-taught and retaught when ramps fall apart, we have to wait our turn, or we need all hands on deck to hold a new ramp in place. This is just one example of how the play centers reinforce what we are learning in other school settings and real life.

Tomorrow, jot down some ideas that can transfer from the classroom to the play center, and how you'll bridge the divide from one setting into the other.

A BLUEPRINT FOR FULL IMPLEMENTATION

Step 1: Locate the right resources.

Once you have established space in your classroom or school for play-based learning, the next step is to find resources to put into the space. Ask around and make sure you're taking your entire team into account on this one. Create a dream wall in a common staff space and have everyone add to it, to seek out what teachers would like to have in the play space. Set up informal and formal focus groups of students to see what they enjoy doing (building, drawing, tinkering, role-playing), and ask preschool centers in your community about which activities have been popular with the classes they served. Getting feedback from your school and local community will help you create a space that is designed for the specific learning you have in mind.

When you review the wish list, make sure what you buy looks like your school community, and the diverse students that you have. Look for grants to find tools, toys, dolls, and posters that look like the students and families you serve. Make sure to send a message that everyone belongs, and enhance the value of family beliefs, rituals, and routines. This sets a foundation of trust and belonging, and gives students a sense of security that is critical to learning.

Step 2: Find the funding.

Now you need to think about funding this work. Apply for grants, save your dollars, and simply ask for help from those around you. Try having a Lego drive, and watch families donate boxes of Legos for your students to use. Local businesses and charities are always eager to support by donating money or purchasing items off a Caring Tree that you could put up during holiday events.

No matter what, setting classroom space aside for students to play has to be the starting point. And call on your teachers to help with the materials. Years of experience in pre-K–3 can directly align to the amount of material the teachers have acquired in their teaching. Teachers new to early learning walk in with few toys and not much money for purchasing more. Those who are more experienced have more in their toolboxes. Collaborate and combine supplies to offer the same experience for all students.

Step 3: Make time to play and learn together.

Play is still important even past 12th grade. For that reason, we offer different opportunities for *staff* to play every year. From our structured professional development to the annual staff Human Hungry Hippo, integrating play into the adults' day reminds us of the importance it can have in our classrooms. It doesn't have to be elaborate, and it certainly doesn't have to take all of your time, but finding little ways throughout the school year to bring play back into the minds of staff will transition into their classrooms as well.

OVERCOMING PUSHBACK

You do *what* in kindergarten? Look, it's a question I get a lot when I'm outside of our school. Dedicating twenty-five minutes per day and two full classroom spaces to play is not globally accepted in elementary programs. Advocating for what is right and what matters for students isn't always easy, either, and at times, it comes with questions and concerns that have to be addressed. Offering "play-dates" so stakeholders can come into your school and experience what play can be is a great starting point. Highlighting play-based lessons or learning outcomes is another way to get parents and community members to support your work. Take videos to document a day of play, and share them via social media to get the word out about the work in your school. Our tagline "Where learning is child's play" is on the note cards we hand out, as a reminder to those who work in our school and those we serve that play is a crucial form of learning for all of us.

Play time is just another prep time for teachers. This isn't even remotely true, because both teachers and students have to actively engage in play-based learning if it's to be successful. Making sure that play time is intentional learning time—and not an additional prep or testing window—is also critical for success. Granted, play is student-directed and independent, and it can be easy to step away and check an email, assess a student, or meet in the corner with another teacher, but it's a leader's responsibility to keep that from happening.

To address this, teachers must uphold clear expectations regarding play center time. Laying these out at the start makes it easier to monitor, observe, and offer feedback later on in the year. Our play center committee spends a great deal of time rotating monthly themes as a way to extend curriculum from the classroom to the play space. Themes for dress-up and reading nooks align with special holidays and events that occur during the year. Allowing the teachers to decide on the tools going into the space gives them the opportunity to fully invest in every second their students spend there.

You can't really count *that* as learning. Enhancing your understanding of the pre-K–3 world means embracing the unique ways in which all students learn. Capturing this learning in a natural setting such as play doesn't diminish this learning. It actually elevates it. Teachers I observe in play-based settings are watching for oral language acquisition, patterning skills, social communication goals being met, and generalization of classroom learning in a different setting. Many teachers go so far as to talk to other district and school leaders, to make them aware of the benefits of play in the early grades, so that this type of learning spreads beyond their respective schools. By intentionally weaving play into a child's school day, you incorporate more ways to learn and document growth—not less.

THE HACK IN ACTION

Teachers come from so many different experiences of play, as do the students, so as an educator, you must find a way to align views and create a common understanding of the importance of play. In our community, we worked to create a professional development day that linked educators from three different settings and asked them to create that common vision.

Play in schools—and that transition to understanding the different views on it—was one of my biggest learning curves as a pre-K/K leader. I had no clue how incredibly important it was to schedule and prioritize play in a child's day. I started leading in a building under-equipped and uninformed on the critical importance of embedded play-based learning into a student's educational programming.

> **By allowing teachers to create play spaces that they know are right for kids, and can help them reach academic milestones, you are honoring their craft and judgment, and enhancing the learning environment for all.**

I can remember the day I walked into play centers for the first time. My initial thought was that it was total chaos. Students were all over the room, playing. Some were in the kitchen area, loading and unloading groceries, while a few were across the way, trying on different occupational costumes in the dress-up area. A group of students was building towers with foam blocks, while others were in the "garage" with a container full of cars, moving them up and down ramps they had created—or ones that were already built. And the teacher? She was playing with a small group of students, herself.

I was confused and frustrated, all at the same time. How did we have time to do this every day, and how did it help children learn? Little did I know then how much learning I had to do to fully understand this critical component of the instructional day.

Shortly after my first play center experience, I began to really dig into the world of early learning. I found books, articles, podcasts, and connections with other pre-K–3 school leaders to start to figure this new universe out. What was the importance of self-directed play-based learning in the early years? Why was it important for teachers to model and fade back during opportunities that would enhance social-emotional development? And how did Tinkertoys enhance opportunities to develop and enhance oral language skills in students who had a different home language than English?

After a few days of connecting the dots, I took my new learning back into play centers—this time with a new lens of understanding. I walked into the play centers with eyes wide open, and ears ready to "hear" what I had been reading and learning about. My mindset was far more open and inquisitive. This time, I had background knowledge about the correct room set-up, tools/toys that would be developmentally appropriate, and questioning techniques for students at this age. I knew that social skill development could occur in a space with so much student choice and voice.

And as students walked into the space, I observed how the teacher gave a brief overview of the different stations, as well as a demonstration of tools/toys if they were new to the class. I listened to an interesting conversation at the grocery store where three students—all English language learners—were giggling and making change for the cereal they were going to take home for lunch with their families. I watched closely as a group of students built an elaborate marble run track, and then ran the marble through the course using skills such as velocity and force, while sorting objects by size and dimension. In the dress-up center, I overheard a lengthy play created by three students reenacting a story their teacher had read to them earlier in the day.

By taking the time to immerse myself in early learning, I built a deeper understanding of the critical components play serves to support all students. Now I advocate for play with any other principal I speak to about enhancing their early learning practices.

As leaders, we need to know the ins and outs of our buildings, but to create safe, collaborative environments that encourage risk-taking, we have to be careful not to micromanage. Realizing the importance of play will happen quickest with hands-on learning experiences, rather than just talking or reading about it. And it's important for both students … and adults.

By allowing teachers to create play spaces that they know are right for kids, and can help them reach academic milestones, you are honoring their craft and judgment, and enhancing the learning environment for all.

INVITE YOURSELF OUT
AND INVITE OTHERS IN

Creating coherence between
worlds of early ed and K–12

*"If you want to go fast, go alone. If you
want to go far, go together."*
—AFRICAN PROVERB

THE PROBLEM: TOO MANY SILOS

Historically, there has been a line in the sand between childcare/preschool settings and the K–12 systems. Any attempt at alignment and collaboration between these two worlds comes up against multiple barriers. It's not always an issue of not wanting to connect and collaborate—but rather the question of how to do it. In a 2016 article published in the *AASA School Administrator* magazine, Joanne Quinn and Michael

Fullan defined coherence as "the shared depth of understanding about the nature of the work." When you apply that to pre-K–3, you find an easy definition: Coherence is about creating systems together, to ensure that each child is safe, successful, engaged, and learning.

Shattering the invisible wall between pre-K and the next step starts with finding meaningful connections between both worlds. As a leader, you have the opportunity to be the bridge between these worlds, rather than the gatekeeper.

Coherence isn't about whose job it is, whose toes you are stepping on, or who isn't doing it the right way. When you are truly working together, collaboration, communication, and high expectations for ALL students become the real focus.

Think about it this way: In coaching, middle school sports teams work together with high school coaches to ensure that everything from technique to play calling works together as the players grow. Students are not expected to start over in eighth or ninth grade, so why do we do it to students and their families between pre-K and K? Why not give students an easier—and more successful—transition?

Many elementary schools are starting to incorporate pre-K and four-year-old kindergarten programming right into their school buildings. While this is a great step in the right direction, these programs only touch a small percentage of the students the schools will serve. Finding out where the children are, what they are learning, and who is leading them is critical to establishing a bridge, rather than a barrier, between pre-K and K.

THE HACK: INVITE YOURSELF OUT
AND INVITE OTHERS IN

Shattering the invisible wall between pre-K and the next step starts with finding meaningful connections between both worlds. As a leader, you have the opportunity to be the bridge between these worlds, rather than the gatekeeper. Finding concrete ways to connect the two systems will make a big impact on the students and staff in the school, and provide a venue to learn and grow on your own.

Once you decide to start reaching out to students and families earlier than kindergarten, you must figure out where to go to find them. This can be as easy as gaining a list of community, private, and public preschool and daycare settings. Start small, with emails introducing yourself, and look for opportunities to invite yourself into preschool meetings to connect with daycare and preschool directors face-to-face. After time and relationship building, start to open the door to formal invitations to activities and professional development.

Another example of this collaboration is finding ways to get K–2 teachers into pre-K classrooms, and vice versa. Using a spreadsheet and creative scheduling, I have been able to offer teachers in our school time to go into various preschool settings to observe their literacy block. Then the teachers they observed in the preschool setting came and observed teachers in kindergarten. This fed into a half-day professional development session on alignment of literacy instruction, and primed the pump for conversation, by allowing teachers to see each other in action with students.

Understand that best practice is good practice no matter what the context—and is critical when you are finding common ground between two systems and sets of educators. Learning from each other only helps us improve for the students we serve today, and the ones that will be in our schools tomorrow.

WHAT YOU CAN DO TOMORROW

- **Observe.** Every K through third-grade educator needs to spend time in a preschool or childcare setting to fully understand the development needs of our youngest learners in a realistic setting. It is one thing to read a book (which I am really glad you are doing right now), and a completely different experience to observe the research in action. As a building leader, if you don't know where the feeder pre-K programs are in your community, find out. Invite them in and make arrangements to give a tour of your school— and then invite yourself out and observe *their* setting. The learning starts with the leader, and when you invest in this partnership, everyone wins.

- **Ask questions.** Each day in the world of pre-K, you can learn something new. From funding to curriculum, state ratings, and program audits, the leaders of early learning are instrumental to the success of our students in K–12. Find opportunities to sit down and ask questions. It will help you find ways to complement and extend the work they are doing— instead of reinventing the wheel.

    In our school district, we started to have transition meetings with preschool sites to find out what made learning successful for their students, so that we can do our best to replicate that environment. By creating a series of questions to guide transition conversations (see Image 7.1 below) we can borrow the tools pre-K teachers used with students to build on that foundation as they transition to K. Without these safety nets in place, educators and leaders will spend too much time running around and reactively putting out fires. If they would invest time up front in training, assessments, and direct lessons, they will find more success—and provide more successful environments for their students.

Transition to Kindergarten Information

Teachers/Child Care Providers: Please complete this form for each child attending kindergarten in the fall of 2015. Mrs. Cabeen will be visiting preschool/child care locations to collect the completed forms. We appreciate you taking the time to fill out this form accurately as it will assist in the transition from early childhood to kindergarten.

Child's Name: _____
                       Last   First   Middle

Date of Birth: _____ Nickname: _____ Gender: Male Female

Preschool/Child Care Setting: _____

Length of time in the above program: _____

Please list any special services this child receives/received: _____

Behavioral Considerations:

When involved in classroom/child care learning, this child is: (check all that apply)

_____ easily engaged	_____ slow to engage in activities
_____ usually confident	_____ tentative
_____ playful	_____ serious
_____ focused	_____ easily distracted
_____ persistent	_____ easily frustrated
_____ quick to respond	_____ needs extra time to respond
_____ talkative	_____ quiet
_____ transitions easily	_____ transitions are difficult

Please list and explain any behavior strategies that have been successful with this child. If a behavior plan was developed, please attach a copy. _____

Image 7.1

- **Work together.** Finding meaningful ways to connect and collaborate can be instrumental in building a stronger relationship between these two worlds. Make a list of things to do, such as inviting preschool teachers to visit your schools, meeting their former students, and attending relevant professional development sessions. It shows how much you appreciate the work and dedication they bring to the craft—and the students they serve.

A BLUEPRINT FOR FULL IMPLEMENTATION

Step 1: Ask for ideas.

Finding out what works in your community takes research and feedback from stakeholders. In our community, when we started talking about what makes a child ready for K, we looked at what was already available. Taking Early Childhood Standards from Minnesota, Wisconsin, and California, we created a survey that was pushed out to all pre-K and K teachers in our community. The survey asked them to identify the top ten skills that would prepare students for kindergarten. From that data, I went to meetings to discuss results, and from that feedback, we created the kindergarten readiness kits that we now give to families registering for kindergarten. They receive these the spring before their children start school. This opportunity not only gave all teachers a voice, but showed them how much I valued their voices—and also laid the foundation for future collaboration.

Step 2: Review learning outcomes.

Taking time as a team to review the learning outcomes, not just for the teacher's own grade level but also vertically, is an eye-opening activity. It diffuses any tension between grade levels regarding what they think should be taught, as opposed to what is actually required. In our state, the format for pre-K and K–12 outcomes is very different. Having conversations surrounding how to link the two has been a powerful way to honor the work in the early grades and understand the foundation that is being paved, as well as giving us a way to make our students more successful.

Step 3: Don't forget about special supports.

If you are working solely with teachers, you are missing a huge component. Paraprofessionals, special educators, related service professionals, interventionists, and ELL educators are critical to working with the whole child, and their voices need to be at the table as well. When we moved forward with implementing Zones of Regulation as a Tier 1 social-emotional framework, we made sure to invite, and compensate, our paraprofessionals and related service team members to attend. Once word got out, we also had early childhood teachers and private music educators in attendance. Making sure that all educators felt they have a voice and are valued gave us a comprehensive approach to student success.

OVERCOMING PUSHBACK

We'll just spend the entire time debating. One of the biggest challenges in alignment resides in the mindsets of the sending and receiving teachers. Early learning educators are the most passionate, caring, and compassionate people I have met. But those characteristics can also be a barrier when it comes to having honest conversations about change and alignment across grade levels, school settings, and students. Too many times, I've heard, "Well if only the K teachers would have done that," or, "Why didn't that teacher retain that student?"

If this is going to work, we have to agree to stop disagreeing so that we can start problem-solving. In the spring, I dedicate four days to go out to the different preschool sites and meet with teachers and pre-K directors to complete transition forms on students. Finding out what has worked and where we still have areas of need, and anything else to consider in kindergarten, has been critical in creating a smooth transition from preschool to kindergarten, and has given us a better picture of the students before they set foot in the classroom.

If we all have that foundation before anyone comes through the door, we go from there, no complaints and no regrets, and the work becomes easier. Responses like, "I am not sure I know how to get the student to grade level," or, "These challenging behaviors are something I haven't seen before. I don't know how to reach him," are based in fear, and are unnecessary. Having honest conversations and calling out negative comments is the best way to move forward and work toward success, rather than wallowing in regret.

What if we don't have time? Getting creative with when and how to communicate is critical. We found things like Skype and Google Hangouts, where we connected with other educators in Minnesota and Iowa, to be very successful. Technology shouldn't be the barrier, but the bridge, for creative collaboration. By removing the face-to-face requirement for collaboration, we were able to think big and plan bigger—as well as reach educators across state lines. We even had Facebook groups, where we shared ideas and resources with each other—from snowy day activities to literacy centers. And we all became better teachers because we took the time to creatively reach out to others.

No one else does what I do. Most of us are familiar with the face-to-face observations, and we know how valuable it is to see theory in practice and ask questions. But location, time, and resources can make it difficult. Face-to-face interactions allow master teachers to reflect on their own practices, and share resources with others. But what if that master teacher is two hours away, or across the country? Where can you find that sort of information more readily?

When I started this work, it was difficult. The research was available, but it lacked the practitioner perspective. I read case studies and textbooks on early learning, but struggled to find clear-cut examples of real people getting the work done in schools. I also found that being a connected early learning leader wasn't as easy as it might be in other grades. Outside of Pinterest, social media has become a third- through 12th-grade resource ... *and* a growing resource for our little learners and leaders. I joined Heidi Veal, Katy Phinney, and Nancy Alvarez in moderating #ECEChat as a way to unite and amplify early learning voices on social media, using platforms like Facebook and Twitter. This chat provides a place for deep conversations and resource sharing between some of the most influential and passionate early learning educators you will find anywhere. More and more, early learning educators are pinning, posting, and tweeting ideas and resources that accelerate learning and enhance the standard for all students.

THE HACK IN ACTION

Visible leadership and creating coherence in the world of early learning looks very different than you might imagine. Starting in the winter, I go into the different daycare and preschool settings in the city, and read to classes. This may seem simple, but is actually an incredible opportunity to observe preschool teachers at work, meet students and families, and build relationships with every stakeholder involved.

Each year, our school hosts a pre-K/K professional development day, and we invite all preschools in our area to participate. I work to secure funding for the speakers or activities, and the daycare/ preschool providers offer the invitation to their teams. What we have found is that learning together is so much better. For instance, one year, we focused on the foundational literacy skills all students should have. Our interdisciplinary table teams came up with incredible ways to collaborate on consistent vocabulary for students. Our district preschool director offered training in the phonics program our district uses, and invited private preschool and daycare providers to attend. We partnered with this opportunity by providing DVDs and YouTube links of the kindergarten teachers using this program, so they could share this with families, as well. Our play date professional development was an incredible way to solidify the importance of play, and generate ideas and ways to incorporate play-based learning in intentional ways during the day.

Another creative way in which we have bridged pre-K and kindergarten has been the establishment of our Pack in Training program. Each spring, we work with preschool and daycare providers to identify students who, due to a variety of risk factors, might have a difficult time transitioning to kindergarten. We then invite these students and their families to our summer Packers in

Training class. The program is held for four half days a week, for three weeks, in August. Students are taught by a current preschool and current kindergarten teacher, in a kindergarten classroom, and are given a pre/post assessment on academic and social-emotional skills to determine which is the greatest area of need. The co-taught class covers everything from eating breakfast in the cafeteria to learning how to rotate in reading centers. This also allows a creative co-teaching environment in which teachers from K and pre-K establish solid relationships and get to see how the different school settings and how both roles support learners.

Each year, student volunteers assist the teachers with recess and other routines, and act as additional mentors in the classroom. One of the student volunteers even comes back during the year, to visit and volunteer in the classrooms in which those students ended up.

At the end of the three weeks, the teachers provide extensive notes for the incoming kindergarten students and their teachers. Every year, we see a huge success from this program, from less tears and an easier separation from a caregiver in the morning to increased independence in the different school environments. These three weeks give students a jump-start to success during the school year, and also provide a space to establish partnership between pre-K and K.

Educators can feel isolated, even in a building full of other educators. Providing time and finding opportunities for them to connect not only with the same grade, but with those above and below them as well, is critical in creating a seamless system for students, and support for educators.

Use structured professional development, observations of different settings, and conference calls/online hangouts to start, and begin to build relationships. The more you know about each other, the more you can build and scaffold those experiences across grades.

CHANGE THE CONVERSATION WITH PARENTS

Cultivating strong relationships with all stakeholders

"Parents don't care what you know until they know that you care."
—Search Institute, *Don't Forget the Families* Study

THE PROBLEM: FAMILIES OFTEN FEEL LIKE OBSERVERS IN THEIR CHILD'S LEARNING, RATHER THAN PARTNERS

ONE OF THE more difficult parts of leading at a grade-level center full of kindergarten students is only having one hundred and seventy-four days to make a difference, instill a love and spark of learning that lasts their whole lives, and ensure that they know they have adults that care for them and have high expectations for what they can achieve.

The same holds true of building solid partnerships with parents in that short amount of time. Too often, when a child enters the K–12 system, we shut the door to the experiences and learning that have occurred at home with the child's family. If you are only calling parents when there is a problem, then *that* is the problem.

 How we welcome and end every day with students can also be a great starting point in building relationships with families.

Because when you shut the door on your student's first and most influential teachers, you lose an opportunity to enhance your own teaching, and the child's learning.

Transparency is critical when working with parents, though, so we have to make sure we don't assume we know anything unless we take the time to ask. Of course, it takes time, and might be inconvenient, and certainly the conversation might go in a different direction than we anticipated. But understanding parents' hopes, dreams, and fears for their child is a gift that can't be ripped open. You need to handle that aspect with care. Have conversations about strengths, as well as honesty around struggles early on, to build a foundation of knowledge and trust. Sometimes, our very best intentions for students directly disrupt our relationships with their families. Withholding information or waiting to say something that needs to be said puts up walls between school and home. Instead, encourage your teachers to enter into conversations with parents that put them at the forefront, not backstage, in regard to their child's education.

THE HACK: CHANGE THE CONVERSATION WITH PARENTS

Having your first (or second, or third) child enter the K–12 system can be a milestone in many ways for families ... and for teachers and leaders. Setting the tone for when and how you communicate and build a mutual relationship goes a long way toward establishing trust with the stakeholders you will be serving on the journey. Authentic family engagement is more than a parent night, more than Dads and Donuts, and if you do it well, it will start well before students enter the classroom, and leave a lasting memory well after they leave your school.

How we welcome and end every day with students can also be a great starting point in building relationships with families. In what ways are you intentionally taking time to show care, concern, and empathy for the students in your class? How often are you checking in with families after a difficult time? When do you recognize that student who just seems to be doing the right thing every time you turn around? How do you celebrate every child during the school year—and make sure that the family hears about it as well?

If you have an opportunity to live where you lead, you have the bonus of engaging with future, current, and previous families in your community every day. This is a chance for parents to see that you are more than a principal, and for you to see how much they love being parents. Building relationships with families can occur on Saturdays at the swimming pool during a swim meet, Sundays at church, or at the library when you check out new books after school and see former students studying.

Since I'm a runner, families that see me out and about, training for upcoming races, sometimes even slow down, pull over, or wave and cheer a few words of encouragement when I am out on long runs.

Finding ways to interact with families outside of school (and in something other than your school outfits or suits) helps everyone understand that before we are the title, we are people, and have a commitment to be better for ourselves, our own families, and our school.

A unique part of my own story is that my youngest son was born in Ethiopia, and raised there for the first five years of his life. My priority is to continue to raise him as a bicultural child—one who lives here but has a strong sense of his African heritage. Because of this, I find opportunities to immerse us both in the rich African culture of our local community. We attend African events, spend time in others' homes for meals, and even have him jumping into pickup basketball games with the older guys from our community. This opportunity has not only been a way for him to grow in his own cultural identity, but a gift for me as well. Raising a bicultural child allows me a glimpse into the world of parenting a child in an area where the parents did not go to school themselves. Opening my eyes and ears to the journeys of families who have come into this country, and their hopes and dreams for their children, has allowed me to understand others from an empathetic point of view.

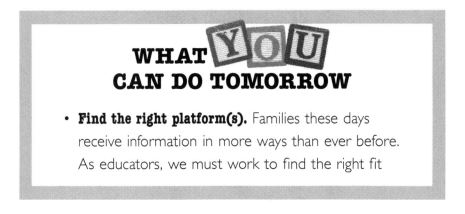

WHAT YOU CAN DO TOMORROW

- **Find the right platform(s).** Families these days receive information in more ways than ever before. As educators, we must work to find the right fit for each family, to make sure they are receiving information in a timely manner. Our school community recognized early on that parents were engaging more with their phones than the school folder. Armed with that information, we created a blog that links directly to our Facebook page. That way, families can see an intro to a subject and click to go right out to the blog for further information. We also post pictures of the school day, host Facebook Live events, and push out reminders on this social platform. I used Twitter and the hashtags #WoodsonK, #PackinTrain, and #wkcrounds so parents can see inside their child's day. YouTube has been a great vehicle for pushing out monthly videos about events as well, and gives families a view into instructional practices that occur every day in kindergarten. Start to put together some ideas, and when you look for what to use, make sure you are surveying your stakeholders so that you are choosing the right tools to reach families, and recognize that there may be more than one right answer.

- **Make sure to teach the tool, and then use it!** Teachers use tools like Seesaw, Remind, Facebook, and Twitter to communicate with their families. Before posting, they spend time at back-to-school conferences, demonstrating the tool and helping families get signed up and logged in. We want to make communication between home and school easy, accessible, and supportive for families. I have even seen teachers highlight the tool during subsequent parent nights and conferences. But once families are signed up, use the tool to communicate early and often. The more you post, the more families practice using it, and the stronger the bridge between home and school will become.

What are some communication tools you can use to communicate? Jot them down— and then start to figure out how you'll pull them into your daily, weekly, and monthly communications.

- **Reach out the old-fashioned way.** One expectation to maintain is that families receive positive communication about their child within the first month of school. Starting the second week of school, armed with addressed postcards and classroom lists, I sit in classrooms and look for the good in everyone. Once I have observed a class, I take the time to write three to five postcards to specific students engaged in learning and positive social behaviors, and/or contributing to class in a specific manner. I use the class list to keep track of who I sent cards to, and then move to the next room. This process takes almost a full thirty days, but is incredibly worth it! Parents and students are proud to receive mail from the principal, and it helps me shift the defined role of what a principal is "supposed" to do to what our vision of school leadership is. Plus I get to contribute to the success of our learners every day!

Starting tomorrow, figure out your own process for positive communication. Make your way into at least one class, observe, and decide how you're going to give the students—and their families—positive reinforcement.

A BLUEPRINT FOR FULL IMPLEMENTATION

Step 1: Be present.

Today, education happens at a very quick pace. We are juggling a hundred things at a time—usually while trying to keep a smile on our faces! Plus, I have found that when parents come to us, they are nervous, intimidated, and/or worried about how we will respond to them. For that reason, I do my very best to be available to families in the various school environments—and to make it painless. My favorite place to be is outside, at parent drop-off/pick-up spots. Parents have a different appreciation for you when they see you greeting their children day after day, helping them out of car seats or handing out hugs and high-fives to everyone that walks by. There is something to seeing the 'boss' of the school (as I have been called by many five-year-olds) in a big fur hat in below-zero temps, soaking wet from snow or rain, or in bright pink hair after the students raised a significant amount of money for cancer research. As a school community, we have taken this part of the day to a new level. Student dismissal in the early grades can be one of the most stressful parts of the day, and making sure students head home as safely as they arrived is a worry for the principal, the parents, and the teachers. Our school deploys everyone for dismissal—classroom teachers and paraprofessionals, interventionists, you name it. We're all there. And this visual presence gives parents a sense of support and an opportunity to connect with teachers outside of the classroom. Teachers report that saying goodbye to students is just as important as greeting them as they arrive, and parents appreciate seeing the red carpet rolled out not just at the beginning, but at the end of each day.

Step 2: Be honest.

Parents want the very best for their kids. Building trust with them takes time and consistency in your responses and actions. Sometimes, being honest is having to say things that are hard to hear. I try my best to call every parent if a child makes an office visit. I start with, "Hello, Mr./Mrs., this is Mrs. Cabeen from Woodson. Could I have a moment of your time?" From there, I talk about what happened and tell them that their child has been to see me, but might not remember all the details. I want to make sure the parents have speaking points, and know the full story.

Now mind you, these incidents are few—and minor—but the feedback I have received usually includes a thank you.

At conference time in the winter, I sit in on conversations for students who are struggling. My role is to be honest and ask for parent support. I usually show visual data (here is where your child is, and this is the target for the end of K), and ask if they can help us. If they can't, that's okay. If they can, we discuss things we need help with (attendance, encouraging a growth mindset for their child, supporting literacy at home). Then we get feedback regarding the ways in which they think they can help make that happen.

If you are concerned about how a conversation might go, ask for help. We have held professional development sessions specifically to talk about responding to hostile emails or social media meltdowns. Teachers share sample emails they have received, and we create responses to these situations as a team, using a framework that defuses the tension rather than escalating it. Many times, teachers use the "phone a friend before hitting send" strategy. If they receive a difficult or direct email, they have another teacher read their response to make sure the message is conveyed the right way. If it's not, they ask for suggestions. Because while it's important to be honest, we also want to make sure we're being gentle, and keeping the student's best interests in mind.

Step 3: Be vulnerable.

Have you noticed how parents tend to let their guards down a little when they learn *gasp* that the teacher or school leader is not … perfect? Parents have seen my own kids running circles around me after multiple attempts to redirect them in the grocery store. They see me apologizing for being pulled/tugged on when I am trying to talk to them at a soccer meet. And, well, they have seen my own kids act in a way that might send them to the principal's office if they were in school! Parents don't want a perfect teacher or principal; they want a person they can relate to—one who has struggles with homework and bedtime, just like everyone else.

OVERCOMING PUSHBACK

What if we don't speak the same language? Too many times, educators forget or don't implement a parent communication channel because of the language differences between school and home. I have had circumstances where teachers were hesitant to contact a parent because they were unsure what language was spoken in the home. Just make the call. Making an attempt to connect with a family, and finding out you need additional help, is better than not trying at all.

As I said earlier, learning how to parent a child from Africa allows me opportunities to make deep connections with our local African community. This has made me more empathetic to what other parents might be going through. Understanding and honoring a family's life experiences, and using the diversity offered, makes the learning space more authentic for everyone involved.

Teachers have very creative ways of providing parents with opportunities to be partners in equipping, engaging, and inspiring their children. I can remember one summer when I gave a tour of the school to a medical researcher from overseas. Her child was coming to our school, while the mother was going to be working full time at the university. Beyond "yes," "no," and "thank you," our language connections were limited—but we were both committed to the tour of the school. She expressed concern that her child wouldn't eat during the school day because he didn't speak English and couldn't communicate his choices. Right away, I knew what to do, and we went into a classroom, where I demonstrated the morning check-in. Each student has a popsicle stick with his or her name on it, and places it in the canister assigned to a food choice for the day. When I was flipping through the pictures, the mom was overjoyed! "Chicken, burger, rice/beans!"

she exclaimed as I turned over each picture. "He knows these and will eat them!" While some reading this might have other ways to have handled the situation, this was a "just at the right time" strategy for me, and helped a nervous parent understand how her child would be able to tell us his basic needs *while* learning English and the school routines.

But parents don't read my weekly newsletter anymore. Teachers' school/home communication tools have gone well beyond paper newsletters on Fridays. Remind, FreshGrade, Seesaw, Facebook, Twitter, blogs, and videos are new ways to enhance and share what is occurring at school. I have watched many parents comment and post on our school Facebook page when their child is featured, as well as sharing with other family members in their home language. Videos about school activities and events also help provide an idea of what our school routines are like and how parents can support and encourage participation. If it is meaningful enough, both schools and parents will find a way to communicate effectively.

What about the war stories? "Oh goodness you have "that" kid in your class? I had the sister." You know the rest. Be cautious about writing a student off before the student even sets foot in the classroom door. It is one thing to be aware of interests, triggers, and important medical needs for your students. It is entirely different to have a fixed mindset about a child, based solely on the family tree. Master teachers approach the new year in two ways. Some will dig deeply into the child's cumulative file to gain knowledge about the student to help the child. Other teachers will wait to open the cumulative file until the first four to six weeks have gone by, so as not to be influenced about who the child is by what the file says. Either way is fine, because it is all about the intention behind the choice. Gathering information to help a situation is very different than using information to create problems.

THE HACK IN ACTION

Julie Bloss (@BlossJulie), elementary principal, is finding that it isn't uncommon for educators to reach out to families through the use of social media. It just makes sense that parents and others enjoy seeing pictures and quick clips of their children participating in activities at school. And with parents being increasingly busy, it sometimes feels as if our best point of contact is through social media. In the past couple of years, Julie has started to "flip" her school's social media presence, and intentionally provide family engagement opportunities. Julie's school uses videos throughout the day to promote skills being taught, and to give families and stakeholders opportunities to see what a day of learning looks like through the eyes of their children. She uses social media to post learning games, show how to practice reading in the car, and give other quick tips for parents to use right away. Using Google Photos, she has students create a video collage of student creations. They take pictures holding artwork so parents can identify their child's artwork right way.

Katy Smith (@KatyMN12), a licensed parent educator and the 2011 Minnesota Teacher of the Year, feels an important first step to engagement is recognizing that not every parent has warm feelings or fond memories of school. Parent engagement efforts are often launched with the parents who always come—the ones with the social capital and positive history with schools, and find it easy to participate. For Katy, working to find ways for *all* families to partner with the schools includes rethinking the traditional conference format. Her conferences have a greeter—someone to welcome families to school and point them in the direction of the classroom—who is genuine, kind, and just the right amount of enthusiastic. She also maintains that conferences need to be relationship-based. Job one for the teacher is to see the parent and child as people. Teachers also need a list of guiding questions, to help them begin to establish a relationship with parents. Here are just a few suggestions:

- Tell me about your son's name. How did you decide on it?

- Your son is in second grade! What do you remember about second grade?

- Now I can see where your daughter gets it! Her _____ is/are just like yours!

- I appreciate _____ about your child. How did you teach him to do that?

- We are working on listening in the classroom; tell me what strategies work for you at home.

- How do you chill out as a family? What helps your child calm down?

- It looks like _____ is crazy about that _____! Tell me the story behind that.

- Building a community in the classroom is important to me. I need lots of helpers to do that. What kinds of skills does your child have to contribute?

- When I need to address misbehavior, what suggestions do you have that will be effective with your child?

- What are your hopes for me as your child's teacher? What are your hopes for your child as my student?

Leading a kindergarten center has many, many rewards—and a few challenges—along the way. One of these is building relationships with families quickly as they enter and exit your building in one school year. Working with five- and six-year-olds really takes a full community to ensure we are making gains for all kids. Building relationships can be messy, and complicated, but is so very worth it.

Our parents' first time on campus can be daunting. Filling out paperwork, confirming vaccination records, and learning about attendance, illness policies, and the structure of the school day is draining—in any language. This process is the one that involves parents most, though, and provides the opportunity to make the K–12 system memorable, and hopefully enjoyable.

To help prepare families for this big event, we created a video in which I play a parent and walk through how to register your child for kindergarten, with captions that explain each step of the process. After parents settle into the gym for a brief talk about vaccinations, length of school day, school supplies, illness, and transportation, we get to the fun stuff. Our Kindergarten Readiness bags are given to every family during registration. During the session, classroom teachers explain how each tool in the bag can support them in preparing their child for kindergarten. From homemade flash cards to a game of Go Fish, each activity comes with a bookmark that explains ideas in English and Spanish for engaging with every child. We also worked with community celebrities (soccer coaches, Sudanese success coach, librarian, city officials) to create videos demonstrating how to play these games, and posted them on YouTube, Facebook, and our parent blog (packersintraining.wordpress.com). From this point forward, we push out information to parents weekly, through videos, articles, and questions. This way, parents have an opportunity to plug into our school six months before it starts.

And it doesn't stop when the school bell rings. Parent Video Newsletter and Facebook posts like #FacesofWoodson provide a glimpse into the school day from the eyes of a child. Parents enjoy our Kid Principal videos, in which we interview five to eight students about their thoughts on school, and post them to YouTube. Every year, we also have a #150WKCchallenge. We give every family a copy of *150 Ways to Show Kids You Care* by Search Institute, and challenge them to complete a mission and post the results on our Facebook page. The results are creative, and encompass the diverse families we serve. Our staff even gets into the challenge and posts their own pictures with their families. Every opportunity to engage families is a gift to our school and students.

So... does it work? I'd like to think so; parents report back to me how their kids are doing in elementary school, and I make sure to reference something specific about their child, and wish them the very best for the year. My husband doesn't necessarily like taking me to the grocery store, as he knows we will get stopped by current and former families giving me updates—and that I'll do my best to listen like it was a member of my own family. It does add some extra time to the trip. Is it worth it? Of course! If you only have one hundred and seventy-four days with a family/child, you have to make every moment count!

Parents are a child's first teacher. They have hopes and dreams bigger than the days or years those students will spend in your classroom or school, and if we don't make an effort to connect their hopes and dreams with the student we are teaching, we have missed an opportunity. Each opportunity missed, every positive phone call not made, and every chance to visit a family passed up is another example of the gap between school and home. We will never have empathy for other families if we refuse to spend time understanding where they are coming from. And without empathy for one another, we lose the opportunity to work together for their children, rather than in isolation.

Having two very different children of my own has given me an opportunity to see what incredible power educators have to influence, motivate, and inspire children—regardless of grade level. Involving parents in this process enhances the chances that the child will grow up and into something bigger and better than anyone ever expected. Establishing strong family partnerships is always worth the risk, as the reward is great.

START LEADING PROFESSIONAL DEVELOPMENT THE WAY YOU WANT STUDENTS TO LEARN

Encouraging creativity, risk-taking, and innovative professional development

"Innovation comes when we're uncomfortable."
—ADAM WELCOME AND TODD NESLONEY, AUTHORS OF *KIDS DESERVE IT!*

THE PROBLEM: ONE-SIZE PROFESSIONAL DEVELOPMENT FITS NO ONE

JUST BECAUSE MOST of us survived the desks in rows and lecture-style learning as students doesn't mean it is the best way to learn as adults. Professional development can't be just sit and get, and differentiation is critical, especially in pre-K through sixth-grade campuses.

I remember teaching in a self-contained K–3 special education classroom. Our professional development was definitely a one-size-fits-all approach. We all sat through third- through sixth-grade testing requirements, and on the flip side, those third- through sixth-grade teachers sat through phonics training that was really maxed out in impact by third grade. While there is time for the same, the adults greatly benefit from differentiation of professional development. They need something that aligns with the needs of the students in their classroom, rather than sessions that are for teachers four grades above or two grades below.

When looking to include pre-K teachers in PD with elementary staff, we must find activities that have a direct impact on their work, and offer opportunities to collaborate vertically, in ways that positively impact all educators.

Changing up how we learn together starts small, but grows into opportunities to change classroom instruction based on professional development. I really disliked how our staff meetings were run when I first got to Woodson. They went on for an hour and there was a great deal of nuts-and-bolts topics and talking at staff. If there was time to discuss anything, it revolved around field trips, parties, and holiday programs—not student achievement.

The change started small, when our PBIS team received a monthly journal prompt that aligned with our staff wellness initiative. Then it grew into something we were doing every month, when a different school committee led us through activities that deepened our understanding of concepts directly applicable in our classrooms. Then, from interpreting the assessments for ELL students to applying explicit vocabulary instruction that matched the learner, to hands-on practice in the gym, activities became something driven by teachers. And they were bringing things up that *they* wanted to talk and learn about. Make and take sessions are still the topic of choice at Woodson. From Dr. Jean to teacher-created math learning centers, make and takes are successful because they are opportunities to collaborate with each other and ask questions prior to implementation.

At the beginning of the school year, each committee in our school signs up to flip a staff meeting with an idea or passion from their committee work. Staff is front-loaded via an article or video, and asked to bring artifacts to the meeting. The teachers develop and implement the PD from start to finish, and everyone leaves with a deeper understanding of the content and how to best implement and incorporate new concepts into the instructional day.

When we scaled Zones of Regulation to a school-wide core social-emotional support, we had a make and take toolbox session. Teachers and paraprofessionals laughed, talked, and laminated their Zones of Regulation boards, student name charts, and ideas for self-regulation. By the end of the session, they had all they needed to teach the next day, and didn't need to take anything home to prep. Honor teachers' time by being honest about their learning and practicing during the day—rather than on their own.

Innovative learning for our students should start with how we lead adults. By providing open-ended edcamp or flipped PD, we can model for adults what we want to see for our students. Continuing to lead in the ways we grew up learning, on the other hand, perpetuates stigma and stalls growth for everyone.

THE HACK: START LEADING PROFESSIONAL DEVELOPMENT THE WAY YOU WANT STUDENTS TO LEARN

If we want to walk into classrooms and see excited, engaged learners floating around the room, having conversations around specific topics of interest, we need to make sure we are defining learners as children ... and adults. Stop providing one-size-fits-all PD, and look for ways to find out what people actually need. Then give them opportunities and time for doing it. Take a look at your current staff meeting format. Is it all sit and get? Does everyone sit and face a speaker, with almost no group discussion, and then only around the questions the speaker provides? Try changing the agenda just a bit. We first started using our Friday Focus as the way to get the nuts and bolts out to everyone, so that it also reached our non-certified staff. That freed up twenty minutes of our meeting, which we now give to the various special committees in the building. They get to showcase a new tool, a new teaching strategy, or new ideas that teachers can use tomorrow to enhance an area of practice.

All professional development must also have a measurable outcome. When we decided to upgrade all our interactive display boards, the heavy work came two years before the new devices. By contracting with the company who sells the boards, we created personalized PD around learning the new boards, and amplifying the ways we could use them. Teachers were put into teams and offered challenges to be completed during the half-day professional development session that was offered multiple times throughout the year. All artifacts created were then showcased to the other teams, in a rotating small-group format, and finally posted to our shared Microsoft OneNote, for archiving and using throughout the year.

 You would be surprised at the talent within your school walls—and utilizing it will help you enhance everyone's understanding about a topic.

Outcomes need to be not only measurable, but also achievable. Notice in the example above that I didn't state that everyone would become advanced-level masters of the new devices. I stated that everyone would work together to create artifacts that were shared with all teachers, and used within the classrooms during the year. Knowing that all teachers have different passions and skill sets, I worked with them to move their knowledge on their personal continuum, rather than the continuum others had set. This was as important as the learning itself.

WHAT YOU CAN DO TOMORROW

- **Find out what people want to learn about.** Review your site team and discuss with site leadership what topics you haven't touched on that people want to learn more about. Flexible seating, Bloom's taxonomy, play-based learning, coding—generate a list and start crowdsourcing. You would be surprised at the talent within your school walls—and utilizing it will help you enhance everyone's understanding about a topic.

- **Intentionally leave open space.** Joe Sanfelippo (@Joe_Sanfelippo) and Tony Sinanis (@TonySinanis) state in their book *Hacking Leadership* that we should "give people time to learn together—with each other and from each other."

  If you are implementing a new idea, block out reflection time after the group time so that staff can go back and digest everything on their own, and make it work for their room and their students. For example, if your site plan includes implemented, student-driven Smart Board lessons, create professional development that allows for team time to go back and create lessons before the end of the session. Find ways to share the learning across grades and teams, so that all teachers can access the work that was created.

- **Empower others to lead.** Early learning leaders can be the least equipped to lead the professional development. Stepping back and allowing classroom leaders to step forward ensures that the work will be deep and meaningful for those participating, and allows the principal to be the learner. It also gives the teacher a chance to lead. When teachers express interest in attending a conference in this system, they know that the expectation will be to come back and share their learning with the rest of us. This has been rolled out as make and takes, role-plays, and sharing of electronic resources that the teacher created after the conference. Adding the expectation that when someone goes out to learn, they will bring something back for the rest of us, means that the dollars we spend are better invested and give us a greater return.

  Take a look at where you have teachers asking

to do conferences and classes this year. Where can you allow those teachers to come back and teach the rest of the staff, or share important tips? Set this idea up in advance so that everyone knows what they're getting into—and what they're going to get out of it.

A BLUEPRINT FOR FULL IMPLEMENTATION

Step 1: Find relevant and timely professional development.

During your check-in with new teachers, pay attention. Do they mention an interest in social media, flexible seating, classroom management, or reading centers? Whatever the interest or passion, find a way to give them opportunities to develop and learn more about this aspect of teaching. Try to find conferences or workshops geared toward new teachers (I Teach K, What Great Educators Do Differently, state PBIS, or state kindergarten conference) and send a team, principal included. It is important to model that as adults, we are never, ever done learning, and attending something together shows your own interest in developing teachers to become better.

During the course of the school year, we offer Appy Hours and other opportunities for educators to virtually connect with other teachers. I have hosted Twitter parties at my house to help staff feel comfortable jumping into chats. We have also created private Facebook groups with other kindergarten teachers in the state and regionally, as a way to share practices and grow in our understanding of key early learning concepts.

Step 2: Model PD that allows for risk-taking and creativity.

During our play-center-flipped staff meeting, teams spent time in different learning centers, creating a series of questions that aligned with Bloom's taxonomy. These were posted above the centers for the month. The next year, we had a "PD in PJ" opportunity in which we had Lego Bingo, Hour of Code, and Bee-Bot Challenges for teachers to navigate through, while reflecting on how these tools could be used in daily instruction. Most recently, we bridged our learning with others and created a pre-K through fourth-grade play date, and invited a local elementary school and four other pre-schools to spend a half day making, coding, creating, and playing.

Step 3: Reframe, reframe, reframe.

When the going gets tough, we need to find new tools in our toolbox to keep going. In preparing for our first coding PD session, I remember sitting next to our math interventionist and tinkering around with code.org. He was flying through the lessons while I was stuck—and frustrated. Even as the school leader, modeling this form of risk-taking was challenging, frustrating, and a struggle for me. Walking into something and being willing to fail in front of others is a huge risk, regardless of your role in the school. But during my leadership professional development, I was introduced to the process of reframing, and how changing your mindset can change your outlook on a situation. The idea is to have fun, listen, be present in the moment, and not worry about failing.

During a tense technology training, after which teachers were going to go out and create lessons on a new platform, we set up a reframing activity to set the stage. Each team of teachers had a physical "gift" in front of them. The goal was to open a gift, read it aloud, and look at a situation from a different angle. Teachers opened gifts such as copy machine down, head lice in the classroom, and a major flu outbreak … for the third time.

The responses to this activity were laughter and very creative and positive outlooks on situations that in the moment, in isolation, can be very draining. But allowing more time for us to reframe and change our outlook, meant we could offer more creative solutions, which meant we'd be able to address these situations with less fear, and better learning opportunities for our students.

Step 4: Remember, it starts with you.

As a teacher or a leader, in order to implement a new way of learning, it is critical that you get behind the movement yourself. Teaching coding club was an intentional way for me to learn *with* students while modeling the opportunity to find new ways to reach them. Even when those ways were not around when I went to school. Whatever you're learning, make sure the principal is part of the journey, rather than existing in a separate space or just sitting in the office!

Step 5: Realize that making mistakes is part of the journey.

Modeling and sharing your mistakes with others is an important part of learning. When we focus too much on the end product rather than the process, we are missing a key part of learning. And we're missing out on something that we look for in our own classrooms. So we're not treating PD the way we treat the learning we expect of our students. And we need to change that. Every November, I am the music teacher for the entire school. That means that for one month, or thirty-six full thirty-minute practices, and two concerts, I am on stage, teaching something that is little more than a distant memory for me. And during those thirty-six practices, I make multiple mistakes. I forget a part of the lyric, miss a cue, or most recently, have my technology go out mid-song (those poor students and teachers listened to me squeak out the last verse of "Snow Pants" while trying to figure out what happened). I used to stress so much about the end product that I missed the opportunity to reflect on the process. Now, after each practice, I follow up with a few teachers and students to talk about the learning that occurred. I try to recognize students who paid extra attention during a piece, or helped a neighbor along. And I don't take myself so seriously anymore, because showing that I make mistakes as well is a very transparent invitation for each teacher and student to feel comfortable doing the same.

At the end of the day, as long as we're all learning, that's all that counts.

OVERCOMING PUSHBACK

Making these changes to professional development doesn't come easy—and certainly won't come without a little pushback! But there are a lot of ways to address the questions.

What if it isn't perfect the first time? Promoting risk-taking for students has to be modeled with the adults as well. Making public mistakes or admitting that we aren't perfect in everything we do in school is a hurdle we have to get over to get to the real work of learning together. Many teachers are nervous about trying new technology for fear of breaking it, or not doing it correctly. Working to create the environment where stakeholders don't have to be afraid or ashamed to step outside of what they know is something to work toward. Leading and teaching with a growth mindset has to start with us first, before we attempt to teach others. Admitting that there are hiccups in the learning process is essential for buy-in. Is everything going to work perfectly the first time? No. Is that a reason to quit? Absolutely not.

Why exactly do we need to do this? When making significant changes that will impact professional development, follow the mantra of "If it is that important, it has to be said in more than one way and more than one time." The conversation should start in all leadership teams: PBIS, PLC, and Site Team. Those leaders help to flesh out the ideas and point out where there might be pushback. They take version 2.0 back to their teams for additional feedback, and then it comes back for version 3.0. And throughout all of this, seek communication with the schools that are feeders and receivers of your students, to ensure that whatever you're doing is aligned to what other schools are doing.

Central office staff should always be aware of what you are doing as well, and how it is getting you to your school vision. Finally, roll it out—on a paper that continues to see revisions. Nothing worth working for is perfect at the start, and the sooner you recognize that, the easier the journey becomes.

How is this going to help me or my students? Pushing the envelope on adult learning requires a lot of buy-in, and opportunities for the adults to figure out the "why" behind the work. For example, when creating essential outcomes in the primary grades, try having small groups of teachers break apart standards and review them. This allows them to see the bigger picture of how the work is going to help their students. Play dates and Appy Hours are great ways to let teachers engage with new tools and then talk about how the tools might enhance learning concepts.

Being intentional with teachers every day is just as important as being intentional with your students. The more they know about the why behind the work, the greater the buy-in.

THE HACK IN ACTION

Flexible seating in schools has recently become a topic of conversation with educators across the state, and in the upper grades, I came up with a way to introduce it at our school: by redesigning the staff lounge.

A few of our teachers had been reading about flexible seating and the positive impact of implementing it into their classrooms. At about the same time, I had gone into our staff lounge/staff meeting space and was immediately embarrassed. Tables and chairs were hand-me-downs from other buildings. Many had duct tape on the arms or seats, and tables were leveled by blocks from the play center. How was this space and the furniture in it creating an environment of collaboration, problem-solving, and relationship building? And how was this an environment that invited stakeholders in, without hindering deeper conversations? I realized that we needed to take a good look at where we were existing if we were going to upgrade the space where learning was taking place.

I moved some funds and worked with our facilities director, as well as our curriculum director, and a dream became a plan. Over Thanksgiving break, the custodian and I swapped out the tables and chairs with standing desks, adult-sized rocking chairs, couches, tables, and wobble seats. We cleaned the bookshelves and reshelved them with a variety of professional books, blank journals, Post-it notes, and pens. We even added a curtain so the space could be divided over the lunch hour if we were hosting a data meeting.

Initially, there was a little shock and confusion over the remodel of the space. Some of the staff loved it right away, while others adjusted over time and much explanation. But slowly, the change started to shift the conversation. Staff commented on what seating best fit their needs, and why. We continue to move chairs and tables to match whatever learning is going to happen after school, and have noticed that our space stays cleaner and more organized than ever before.

Then it started. First it was one or two teachers raising their student tables to the very top notch on one table, and lowering another almost to the floor. Individual seating cushions and rocking or cube chairs started popping up in every classroom. And my favorite: Teachers started to make movable student name plates, so the students could decide each day where and how they wanted to sit and learn. By focusing on the adults first, we built an opportunity to see how flexible seating could really impact student learning.

In the end, modeling the learning for adults was critical in helping them understand the application this could take in their own classrooms—and the positive impact it would have on the students they serve.

Warning Elevating professional development by allowing differentiation, self-selection, and opportunities for personal reflection will quickly become favored over traditional forms of sit and get learning. As a successful traditional student myself, I found the release of learning, even with adults, to be scary. However, if we want to offer new learning experiences for the students we serve, we have to start with the adult community.

Utilizing leadership teams to create the learning for adults allows for more feedback and a higher likelihood of success. As educators, we need to equip ourselves and our colleagues with the skills to ensure that all our learners are reaching their highest levels. Creating environments that match the diverse learning needs of all the people in your school offers an inclusive opportunity, and enforces the learning for everyone, no matter what.

MOVE ON UP

Creating sustainable and successful transitions from pre-K through third grade

*"We cannot paralyze ourselves because others are
not doing the things that need to be done.
We must take initiative and be the change, not the same."*
—TODD WHITAKER, JEFFREY ZOUL, AND JIMMY CASAS, AUTHORS OF *START. RIGHT. NOW.*

THE PROBLEM: WE NEED TO LEARN ABOUT OUR STUDENTS WELL BEFORE THEY WALK INTO OUR SCHOOLS

MOVING INTO THE K–12 system is a big milestone for students and their families. It starts their journey of lifelong learning and building relationships around multiple stakeholders in the educational system. If we really want students to be ready for K, then we better be ready to start working with them well before they come to us. This conversation is no longer about whether the students are ready for our school—but about how prepared we are to support the students.

Think about it: So many things change between pre-K and K, including length of school day, cost to attend class, home visits, parent nights, required school attendance, school supplies, recess, academic expectations, homework, and transportation. Expecting preschool teachers, parents, and students to fit into the K–12 expectations without support, guidance, and/or an attempt at working together is unfair to everyone involved.

Learning together and starting early is essential for the work that will lie ahead.

THE HACK: MOVE ON UP

Entering kindergarten shouldn't have to be a hoop-jumping process for anyone. Offering all adults associated with the process an opportunity to ask questions and become experts at enrollment only supports students and families. Make sure the local preschools, Head Starts, and daycare providers have all the information they need for kindergarten registration, as well. Go to daycare meetings and explain the process, and then answer questions about financial requirements for free/reduced lunch, bussing information, and truancy practices for families who struggle with regular attendance. By equipping all leaders of early learning with the information necessary for the transition forward, you'll help to make the process smoother for families and students.

Try to invite yourself to parent nights at preschools as well, to speak to families in their environment rather than yours. We have a community Welcome Center that works with refugee and immigrant families relocating to our community. We give the center the PowerPoint of kindergarten registration, as well as packets of information they can use to help families apply for jobs, rent apartments, and register for school. One year, we even set up tables between shift changes at one of the larger employers, to support families in understanding the process of school registration. It was easier because they didn't have to come to us. We went to them.

Get out there and make those connections. Any time you get an invitation in, say yes. Building strong partnerships starts with saying yes and going to where your future families are.

WHAT YOU CAN DO TOMORROW

- **Invite them in, and invite yourself out.** We've already talked about this one, but it makes sense to talk about it again. Take the time to invest in your students well before they set foot in your school. Make connections with local preschools and daycare providers, and make that an informal but integral part of the transition. I started going and reading to preschoolers as a way to get to know the students, and have found it to be an incredible vehicle for communication with staff and parents. pre-K and daycare providers are far more comfortable approaching me now, and asking about attendance expectations, literacy skills, and techniques to support self-regulation. They use my answers as a way to bridge their students from earlier programs up into kindergarten.

- **Learn together.** Extending an invitation to relevant professional development has also been a way to strengthen our vertical conversations from pre-K through fourth grade. We have invited public and private preschools to at least one professional development session per year. One year, it was a half-day workshop and collaboration about ways to support early learners with skills to develop oral language. Another year, we included Neveln Elementary, a feeder first- through fourth-grade school, as well, and had a pre-K through fourth-grade maker/coding and play date. All teachers were grouped vertically, and set to complete challenges and have discussions around the necessary play skills and how those learning opportunities could be woven into classrooms of four-year-olds *and* fourth graders.

  Come up with some ideas about how to connect with other educators, and how to cross grades in your learning. The more learning you do together, the better you'll be able to serve students across grades as they move up.

- **Review, revise, repeat.** Review what you're already doing, and figure out how it's working. During the first week of school, I make time to connect with teachers to see if the transition forms we collected were helpful, or if I should add/delete/change questions. We review the assessment data from the registration day to determine its validity, and teachers also provide direct feedback from their back-to-school conferences. We look at the content we share and determine whether there is a way to make the experience more meaningful and supportive for families. Documenting all these changes and ideas is critical, because by the time you want to implement new programs, the small details have become lost in a sea of teaching and learning with little ones.

A BLUEPRINT FOR FULL IMPLEMENTATION

Step 1: Create a team.

Successful transitions cannot occur in isolation. Working as a team and using a framework to guide conversations is critical if you want to ensure you have a plan that supports the different needs of students and families. One tool we have used is the NAESP-created guide entitled *Leading pre-K–3 Learning Communities*. This guide provides different competencies, questions, resources, and schools doing the work as a model for moving forward. As a district, create a pre-K–3 team that includes a curriculum director, early childhood coordinator, elementary principal, and teachers. This comprehensive team dynamic allows you to think about transitions from the lens of each stakeholder, and provides a far more developed plan. Work as a collaborative, dynamic team to find a framework for pre-K–3 alignment and leadership that works for your community. And seek stakeholders that represent your diverse community needs, and who have a commitment to seeing your youngest learners become your community's greatest leaders.

Step 2: Meet regularly and often.

This work is critical, so make the time for it. Maintain regular meetings, action plans, and focused action steps for moving the work forward. Set aside time to meet with stakeholders at locations and times that are convenient for everyone. Create action plans and follow up on them, to build a sense that what you are focusing on matters. What is your community's vision for all students? How can that vision be firmly planted in all three- to five-year-olds? Ensure that you have the voice of the students, families, and other community stakeholders woven into all aspects of your plan. In our community, we are fortunate to have a nonprofit organization to partner with on this work. Austinaspires.org holds meetings with community stakeholders passionate about ensuring that all children in Austin are ready for kindergarten and beyond. This action team worked to create a series of kindergarten readiness skills, and posts them throughout the community, as well as creating kits to hand out to families. This approach is a strong reminder that it is not just one person or one school that is responsible for preparing students. It is a community-wide effort that makes the biggest difference.

Step 3: Document the work.

Spending the time meeting with and learning about students requires documentation, which guarantees consistency between the systems and schools. Working with a principal intern, we created a transition form for students transitioning from pre-K to K. During our registration event, we ask families for permission to go to their child's preschool to gain information about their child's learning styles, personality, and anything else that will make the transition a smooth and successful one. Once we have identified the students and their preschools, we send the forms out for teacher feedback. About one month later, I go out to the sites and meet with the teachers to go over the forms and gain any additional details. At the same time, kindergarten teachers are completing the same forms for their students heading to first grade. Putting the work in writing adds value to the educators, and provides a way to ensure that the students move up seamlessly.

Step 4: Celebrate the small successes.

Did you recently have a pre-K–3 staff development opportunity? How about a parent group at your community preschools, where they talked about kindergarten readiness? Or have you developed a common vision of pre-K–3 with key stakeholders? Too often, we fix one thing and move on to the next without taking the time to reflect on what we learned and how we grew from the success. Eating the elephant of school success for all comes one bit at a time, and that needs to include pausing during the journey to reflect on the learning, remind us where we started, and look ahead to where we are going.

Celebrate it! Share it! Once you have started the work, grow on it.

OVERCOMING PUSHBACK

It isn't my job. Sometimes, looking forward means taking a few steps backward first—and doing something that you might not think of as your real job. Educators who assume responsibility of the learning only when the child is in a seat in their class miss an opportunity to build trust and a relationships with those students years before they set foot in their school or classroom. One of my favorite jobs during conferences is as resident child care provider. If you need me on those nights, I will be in someone's classroom, holding a student's baby brother or sister. This is an opportunity for the parent to be fully engaged in the conversation about their child in school—and a chance for me to form a small relationship with a child who will come to this school four to five years later. So many of our requests for teachers come from this place of comfort and care. Teachers will admit that they have an entire family of students within a five- to ten-year period, and some of us are working on the next generation already. Spending time with children and ensuring that they and their families know you care will have a lasting impact on their perceptions of you and your school.

How do we avoid the blame-shifting? When a student comes into the school year struggling, you have two options: blame the people before you, or honor the work that has been done and more forward. Nothing comes from placing blame on others, besides hurt feelings and misunderstandings. Taking time to thank those that worked before you to support the students you now serve is a wonderful way to build relationships and show gratitude. During the fall, I take time to send cards to the local preschools to thank them for the class of students they gave us, and point out how well they prepared them for our school. This small gesture goes a long way in showing gratitude for educators who do the heavy lifting, well before our students get to the primary grades.

What if preschools don't respond? If you want to create opportunities for collaboration and transparency, sharing goes a long way. Don't make others recreate a wheel you worked really hard on. For example, if your school is having positive successes with a social-emotional curriculum, tell the schools who have students in the same grades, and younger. As a leadership team, if you have found the critical pre-academic skills students would benefit from having before they enter your school, don't just email it to the preschools. Set up times to meet with them, and review and demonstrate ways that it could be worked on in their settings. The last thing anyone needs is to find the answer to a problem, only to learn that the person holding the key won't open the box.

THE HACK IN ACTION

As I have said before, one hundred and seventy-four days of kindergarten go by really fast. Right after our holiday program, the school secretary dives into census data to start finding all the children who will be five by September 1, to invite their families to registration in March! And at the same time, we start to create plans for transitioning from K to first grade as seamlessly as possible.

This starts with reviewing our behavior data. In the spring, we pull the names of students who have had three or more major behaviors and five or more minor behaviors to see if interventions during the course of the year have been successful—or if more changes need to be made. Once the list is refined, we identify those students with a notation on the first-grade spreadsheet, so when we start the clustering process, we don't place all of them in one room. Next comes feedback from the specialists. ELL teachers give guidance based upon the spring assessments, our math/reading interventionists offer suggestions, and the gifted and talented interventionist shares lists of students who are reading well above grade level.

Once that information is received, we start to identify which schools each child will be attending, and share that information with the current kindergarten teacher. Then, teachers spend time looking over the lists and making notes about students who have worked well together, and other students that might be best to separate for the upcoming year. Using teacher reports and parent requests, the district data coordinator, instructional coach, and I lock ourselves in a room and begin the clustering process. Using academic and behavioral data, along with feedback from current teachers, we make sure the receiving elementary principals have class lists that have been carefully reviewed and created for everyone's best success.

Any student who was referred to our RtI team is also flagged on the spreadsheet, to indicate that there is additional documentation for the first-grade teacher. This file might include social stories, point sheets, communication logs, or visual schedules that were put in place during the school year with success. Behavioral data is included, so teachers can have a sense of the function of behaviors, and interventions are aligned to need. In some cases, we will even invite the first-grade teachers or principals for a visit, to meet specific students as a way of easing the process for all parties involved.

 **Taking the time to map out transition plans with students and families enhances the trusting relationship before the students even step foot in your school.**

And just as we got forms from pre-K teachers, our kindergarten teachers fill out forms on specific students and send them to the first-grade teachers. These might be as simple as supports for the first days of school, or as detailed as the check-in/check-out process used on another child. Our motto is "If it worked, share it forward." Because once the students leave us, we don't see them on a daily basis. But we want to equip the receiving teacher with everything and anything that will make the transition easier.

For us, the pre-K through fourth-grade play date was an opportunity to get local preschools, the kindergarten center, and a local elementary school together to start the conversation within the ages of three through fourth grade. A leadership team was established to determine what the baseline of understanding was at each site regarding the importance of play. From there, the team created pre-work for all participants, as a way to walk in with foundational knowledge of play in any grade.

The team also created three separate modules for vertical teams (pre-K through fourth grade) to rotate through during the day. One module was a challenge to use play tools to enhance a literacy lesson; the next module was a chance for educators to use robots, coding programs, and games to enhance computational thinking in pre-K through fourth grade; and the third module was a team challenge in a makerspace environment. To enhance the day, we applied for and received a grant from a local education collaborative to provide each school with materials they could take back and use the next day, based upon the conversations and play the adults engaged in. The immediate feedback was incredible. Teachers actually groaned when their time was up in the space! Vertical teams (pre-K through fourth grade) responded positively to the fact that the teams crossed grades and multiple schools. Having time to connect and understand the vertical implications of play in an informal space was time well spent.

This is a critical time in a young person's life, because there are many transitions. From life at home to daycare, preschool, or kindergarten, the transitions are big and important. The adults surrounding the students have the responsibility to make sure that they have created systems that wrap around students and their parents.

Meeting with those involved in the transitions, and asking how the process could be smoother, allows you to really see the process from their eyes. Families from any background all want the same thing: to ensure that their child has better opportunities and better outcomes in life than they had themselves.

Taking the time to map out transition plans with students and families enhances the trusting relationship before the students even step foot in your school. And by honoring and appreciating the work that the team before you has put into the students, you will continue to build trusting relationships with everyone involved.

CONCLUSION
Loving the sandbox

"Children don't have to come from you,
sometimes they just come through you."
—FROM THE MOVIE *COLLATERAL BEAUTY*

My INITIAL TRANSITION from middle school to kindergarten was difficult. I walked in thinking I had the necessary skills to lead at the early level ... and within minutes I was proven wrong on every account. The work and learning curve I needed to be successful were challenging and time intensive. The research and book lists were long, the conferences, podcasts, and Twitter chats were full of ideas—so much so that my brain hurt at times. Developing a collaborative school culture built on trust and high expectations for all was exhausting.

Leading and learning at a school as a principal and a parent provides a unique lens to learn from. Not only did I make decisions based on research, but from the perspective of "How will this enable my son to achieve at high levels all through his school year?" I had a deeper passion to find ways to ensure that my son, his friends, and his peers were achieving at high levels by all means, because I had a personal investment in the work. I now have a greater understanding that with excellent teaching, appropriate programming, and strong parent connections, anything can be achieved by dreaming big—starting right away.

My final piece of advice is this: Choose one thing, do it well, and move on to the next. If you are new to this work, it can seem overwhelming. Start small, build success, and go from there. It could be observing in a classroom, it could be helping in the cafeteria. See a need, fill it, and watch your capacity for more grow.

As much as I truly love middle school students, if I was given the option to go back to middle school today, I am not sure I could leave this new place I have called home. Watching the early development of a child is a gift many elementary leaders don't realize they are blessed to witness. Every year, I watch teachers work with students who have not experienced any form of school, and within weeks these children are able to follow school routines and take turns—and all with an excitement of learning that is truly magically. I look forward to watching my first class of kindergarten students graduate from our high school in less than seven years. I can't wait to see how many "grand principal" children I will have again next year (this year I am up to five), and with each generation comes a new opportunity to set the stage for a successful K–12 career.

I certainly hope you have enjoyed reading this book as much as

I love living it every day. This work can be heartbreaking, heart-wrenching, and completely fulfilling—all in the same day.

Dream big, live colorfully, and lead boldly!

—JESSICA

OTHER BOOKS IN THE
HACK LEARNING SERIES

HACKING EDUCATION
10 Quick Fixes For Every School

By Mark Barnes (@markbarnes19) & Jennifer Gonzalez (@cultofpedagogy)

In the bestselling *Hacking Education*, Mark Barnes and Jennifer Gonzalez employ decades of teaching experience and hundreds of discussions with education thought leaders to show you how to find and hone the quick fixes that every school and classroom need. Using a Hacker's mentality, they provide **one Aha moment after another** with 10 Quick Fixes For Every School – solutions to everyday problems and teaching methods that any teacher or administrator can implement immediately.

"Barnes and Gonzalez don't just solve problems; they turn teachers into hackers—a transformation that is right on time."

—DON WETTRICK, AUTHOR OF *PURE GENIUS*

MAKE WRITING
5 Teaching Strategies That Turn Writer's Workshop Into a Maker Space

By Angela Stockman (@angelastockman)

Everyone's favorite education blogger and writing coach, Angela Stockman, turns teaching strategies and practices upside down in the bestselling, *Make Writing*. She spills you out of your chair, shreds your lined paper, and launches you and your writer's workshop into the maker space! Stockman provides five right-now writing strategies that reinvent instruction and **inspire both young and adult writers** to express ideas with tools that have rarely, if ever, been considered. *Make Writing* is a fast-paced journey inside Stockman's Western New York Young Writer's Studio, alongside the students there who learn how to write and how to make, employing Stockman's unique teaching methods.

"Offering suggestions for using new materials in old ways, thoughtful questions, and specific tips for tinkering and finding new audiences, this refreshing book is inspiring and practical in equal measure."

—Amy Ludwig VanDerwater, Author and Teacher

HACKING ASSESSMENT
10 Ways to Go Gradeless in a Traditional Grades School

By Starr Sackstein (@mssackstein)

In the bestselling *Hacking Assessment,* award-winning teacher and world-renowned formative assessment expert Starr Sackstein unravels one of education's oldest mysteries: How to assess learning without grades—even in a school that uses numbers, letters, GPAs, and report cards. While many educators can only muse about the possibility of a world without grades, teachers like Sackstein are **reimagining education**. In this unique, eagerly-anticipated book, Sackstein shows you exactly how to create a remarkable no-grades classroom like hers, a vibrant place where students grow, share, thrive, and become independent learners who never ask, "What's this worth?"

"The beauty of the book is that it is not an empty argument against grades—but rather filled with valuable alternatives that are practical and will help to refocus the classroom on what matters most."

—ADAM BELLOW, WHITE HOUSE PRESIDENTIAL INNOVATION FELLOW

HACKING THE COMMON CORE
10 Strategies for Amazing Learning in a Standardized World

By Michael Fisher (@fisher1000)

In *Hacking the Common core,* longtime teacher and CCSS specialist Mike Fisher shows you how to bring fun back to learning, with 10 amazing hacks for teaching all core subjects, while engaging students and making learning fun. Fisher's experience and insights help teachers and parents better understand close reading, balancing fiction and nonfiction, using projects with the core, and much more. *Hacking the Common Core* provides **read-tonight-implement-tomorrow strategies** for teaching the standards in fun and engaging ways, improving teaching and learning for students, parents, and educators.

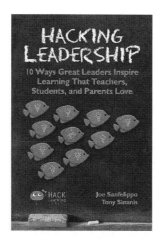

HACKING LEADERSHIP
10 Ways Great Leaders Inspire Learning That Teachers, Students, and Parents Love

By Joe Sanfelippo (@joesanfelippoFC) and Tony Sinanis (@tonysinanis)

In the runaway bestseller *Hacking Leadership*, renowned school leaders Joe Sanfelippo and Tony Sinanis bring readers inside schools that few stakeholders have ever seen—places where students not only come first but have a unique voice in teaching and learning. Sanfelippo and Sinanis ignore the bureaucracy that stifles many leaders, focusing instead on building a culture of **engagement, transparency, and most important, fun**. *Hacking Leadership* has superintendents, principals, and teacher leaders around the world employing strategies they never before believed possible.

"The authors do a beautiful job of helping leaders focus inward, instead of outward. This is an essential read for leaders who are, or want to lead, learner-centered schools."

—George Couros, Author of *The Innovator's Mindset*

HACKING LITERACY
5 Ways To Turn Any Classroom Into a Culture Of Readers

By Gerard Dawson (@gerarddawson3)

In *Hacking Literacy*, classroom teacher, author, and reading consultant Gerard Dawson reveals 5 simple ways any educator or parent can turn even the most reluctant reader into a thriving, enthusiastic lover of books. Dawson cuts through outdated pedagogy and standardization, turning reading theory into practice, sharing **valuable reading strategies**, and providing what *Hack Learning Series* readers have come to expect—actionable, do-it-tomorrow strategies that can be built into long-term solutions.

HACKING ENGAGEMENT
50 Tips & Tools to Engage Teachers and Learners Daily

By James Alan Sturtevant (@jamessturtevant)

Some students hate your class. Others are just bored. Many are too nice, or too afraid, to say anything about it. Don't let it bother you; it happens to the best of us. But now, it's **time to engage!** In *Hacking Engagement*, the seventh book in the *Hack Learning Series*, veteran high school teacher, author, and popular podcaster James Sturtevant provides 50—that's right five-oh—tips and tools that will engage even the most reluctant learners daily.

HACKING HOMEWORK
10 Strategies That Inspire Learning Outside the Classroom

By Starr Sackstein (@mssackstein) and Connie Hamilton (@conniehamilton)

Learning outside the classroom is being reimagined, and student engagement is better than ever. World-renowned author/educator Starr Sackstein has changed how teachers around the world look at traditional grades. Now she's teaming with veteran educator, curriculum director, and national presenter Connie Hamilton to bring you **10 powerful strategies** for teachers and parents that promise to inspire independent learning at home, without punishments or low grades.

"Starr Sackstein and Connie Hamilton have assembled a book full of great answers to the question, 'How can we make homework engaging and meaningful?'"

—DOUG FISHER AND NANCY FREY, AUTHORS AND PRESENTERS

HACKING PROJECT BASED LEARNING
10 Easy Steps to PBL and Inquiry in the Classroom

By Ross Cooper (@rosscoops31) and Erin Murphy (@murphysmusings5)

As questions and mysteries around PBL and inquiry continue to swirl, experienced classroom teachers and school administrators Ross Cooper and Erin Murphy have written a book that will empower those intimidated by PBL to cry, "I can do this!" while at the same time providing added value for those who are already familiar with the process. *Hacking Project Based Learning* demystifies what PBL is all about with **10 hacks that construct a simple path** that educators and students can easily follow to achieve success.

"*Hacking Project Based Learning* is a classroom essential. Its ten simple 'hacks' will guide you through the process of setting up a learning environment in which students will thrive from start to finish."

—Daniel H. Pink, *New York Times* Bestselling Author of *DRIVE*

HACK LEARNING ANTHOLOGY
Innovative Solutions for Teachers and Leaders

Edited by Mark Barnes (@markbarnes19)

Anthology brings you the most innovative education Hacks from the first nine books in the *Hack Learning Series*. Written by twelve award-winning classroom teachers, principals, superintendents, college instructors, and international presenters, *Anthology* is every educator's new problem-solving handbook. It is both a preview of nine other books and a **full-fledged, feature-length blueprint** for solving your biggest school and classroom problems.

HACKING GOOGLE FOR EDUCATION
99 Ways to Leverage Google Tools in Classrooms, Schools, and Districts

By Brad Currie (@bradmcurrie), Billy Krakower (@wkrakower), and Scott Rocco (@ScottRRocco)

If you could do more with Google than search, what would it be? Would you use Google Hangouts to connect students to cultures around the world? Would you finally achieve a paperless workflow with Classroom? Would you inform and engage stakeholders district-wide through Blogger? Now, you can say Yes to all of these, because Currie, Krakower, and Rocco remove the limits in *Hacking Google for Education*, giving you **99 Hacks in 33 chapters**, covering Google in a unique way that benefits all stakeholders.

"Connected educators have long sought a comprehensive resource for implementing blended learning with G Suite. *Hacking Google for Education* superbly delivers with a plethora of classroom-ready solutions and linked exemplars."

—DR. ROBERT R. ZYWICKI, SUPERINTENDENT OF WEEHAWKEN TOWNSHIP SCHOOL DISTRICT

HACKING ENGAGEMENT AGAIN
50 Teacher Tools That Will Make Students Love Your Class

By James Alan Sturtevant (@jamessturtevant)

50 student engagement Hacks just weren't enough. Thirty-three-year veteran classroom teacher James Alan Sturtevant wowed teachers with the original *Hacking Engagement*, which contained 50 Tips and Tools to Engage Teachers and Learners Daily. Those educators and students got better, but they craved more. So, longtime educator and wildly popular student engager Sturtevant is *Hacking Engagement Again*!

"This book is packed with ideas that can be implemented right away: Some creatively weave technology into instruction, others are just plain creative, and all of them are smart. Plus, the QR codes take the reader to so many more fantastic resources. With this book in hand, every teacher will find ways to freshen up their teaching and make it fun again!"

—JENNIFER GONZALEZ, BESTSELLING AUTHOR, SPEAKER, AND CEO AT
CULTOFPEDAGOGY.COM

HACKING DIGITAL LEARNING STRATEGIES
10 Ways to Launch EdTech Missions in Your Classroom

By Shelly Sanchez Terrell (@ShellTerrell)

In *Hacking Digital Learning Strategies*, international EdTech presenter and NAPW Woman of the Year Shelly Sanchez Terrell demonstrates the power of EdTech Missions—lessons and projects that inspire learners to use web tools and social media to innovate, research, collaborate, problem-solve, campaign, crowd fund, crowdsource, and publish. The 10 Missions in *Hacking DLS* are more than enough to transform how teachers integrate technology, but there's also much more here. Included in the book is a **38-page Mission Toolkit**, complete with reproducible mission cards, badges, polls, and other handouts that you can copy and distribute to students immediately.

"The secret to Shelly's success as an education collaborator on a global scale is that she shares information most revered by all educators, information that is original, relevant, vetted, and proven, combining technology with proven education methodology in the classroom. This book provides relevance to a 21st century educator."

—THOMAS WHITBY, AUTHOR, PODCASTER, BLOGGER, CONSULTANT, CO-FOUNDER OF #EDCHAT

HACKING PARENTHOOD
10 Mantras You Can Use Daily to Reduce the Stress of Parenting

By Kimberley Moran (@kimberleygmoran)

You throw out consequences willy nilly. You're tired of solutions that are all or nothing. You're frustrated with the daily chaos. Enter mantras, invaluable parenting anchors wrapped in tidy packages. These will become your go-to tools to calm your mind, focus your parenting, and concentrate on what you want for your kids. Kimberley Moran is a parent and a teacher who works tirelessly to find best practices for simplifying parenting and maximizing parent-child communication. Using **10 Parent Mantras as cues to stop time and reset**, Moran shares concrete ways to parent with intention and purpose, without losing your cool.

HACKING CLASSROOM MANAGEMENT
10 Ideas To Help You Become the Type of Teacher They Make Movies About

By Mike Roberts (@baldroberts)

Utah English Teacher of the Year and sought-after speaker Mike Roberts brings you 10 quick and easy classroom management hacks that will make your classroom the place to be for all your students. He shows you how to create an amazing learning environment that actually makes discipline, rules, and consequences obsolete, no matter if you're a new teacher or a 30-year veteran teacher.

"Mike writes from experience; he's learned, sometimes the hard way, what works and what doesn't, and he shares those lessons in this fine little book. The book is loaded with specific, easy-to-apply suggestions that will help any teacher create and maintain a classroom where students treat one another with respect, and where they learn."

—CHRIS CROWE, ENGLISH PROFESSOR AT BYU, PAST PRESIDENT OF ALAN, AUTHOR OF *DEATH COMING UP THE HILL, GETTING AWAY WITH MURDER: THE TRUE STORY OF THE EMMETT TILL CASE; MISSISSIPPI TRIAL, 1955*

HACKING THE WRITING WORKSHOP
Redesign with Making in Mind

By Angela Stockman (@AngelaStockman)

Agility matters. This is what Angela Stockman learned when she left the classroom over a decade ago to begin supporting young writers and their teachers in schools. What she learned transformed her practice and led to the publication of her primer on this topic: *Make Writing: 5 Teaching Strategies that Turn Writer's Workshop Into a Maker Space*. Now, Angela is back with more stories from the road and plenty of new thinking to share.

"Good writing is good thinking. This is a book about how to think better, for yourself and with others."

—DAVE GRAY, FOUNDER OF XPLANE, AND AUTHOR OF *THE CONNECTED COMPANY*, *GAMESTORMING*, AND *LIMINAL THINKING*

HACK LEARNING RESOURCES

All things Hack Learning:
hacklearning.org

The entire *Hack Learning Series* on Amazon:
hacklearningbooks.com

The Hack Learning Podcast, hosted by Mark Barnes:
hacklearningpodcast.com

Hack Learning on Twitter
@HackMyLearning
#HackLearning
#HackingLeadership
#HackingLiteracy
#HackingEngagement
#HackingHomework
#HackingPBL
#MakeWriting
#HackGoogleEdu
#EdTechMissions
#ParentMantras
#MovieTeacher
#HackingEarlyLearning

Hack Learning on Facebook:
facebook.com/hacklearningseries

Hack Learning on Instagram:
hackmylearning

The Hack Learning Academy:
hacklearningacademy.com

MEET THE AUTHOR

Jessica Cabeen is the principal of the "Happiest Place in Southeastern Minnesota": the Woodson Kindergarten Center. She has been an assistant middle school principal, a special education supervisor, and special education teacher.

She started her career as a music therapist and worked with adults with disabilities and adolescents in residential settings in Iowa and Illinois. She holds a bachelor's degree in music therapy from the University of Wisconsin-Eau Claire, a master's degree in special education from the University of St. Thomas, and her administrative licenses from Hamline University.

Jessica was awarded the NAESP/VINCI Digital Leader of Early Learning Award in 2016, and in 2017 was named the Minnesota National Distinguished Principal. Jessica is active on social media (@JessicaCabeen) and co-moderates #ECEChat, as well as engaging with other educators looking to make all things possible for our young learners, and learners that are young at heart.

She enjoys quality time at home with her husband Rob, as well as her two sons, Kenny and Isaiah. You can reach out to her at www.jessicacabeen.com.

ACKNOWLEDGEMENTS

THIS BOOK WOULD not have been possible without the incredible people in my life who have shared their stories, hearts, and dreams for themselves, their students, and children with me throughout the years. So in true kindergarten fashion ...

A *round of applause* to Mark Barnes, Kelly Schuknecht, and Carrie White-Parrish. Each of you has been instrumental in putting my thoughts into words.

A *huge air hug* to the students, staff, and families of the Woodson Kindergarten Center. Thank you for trusting me to learn and lead alongside some of the most incredible people, who I am honored to work alongside every day.

A *virtual high-five* to my incredible PLN! From tweets to texts, Voxer messages, phone calls, and real-life meet-ups, I have become exponentially better because of each of you.

And finally, *happy tears* for the ongoing support of my close friends and family.

Kenny, you show me the importance of being a kind and compassionate person every day. Isaiah, your persistence, drive, and smile have taught me to never give up, and to always have hope. And Rob, I am so grateful that you continue to support all my crazy, wild ideas, and always believe in me more than I do myself.

—JESSICA

PUBLICATIONS

Times 10 is helping all education stakeholders improve every aspect of teaching and learning. We are committed to solving big problems with simple ideas. We bring you content from experts, shared through multiple channels, including books, podcasts, and an array of social networks. Our mantra is simple: Read it today; fix it tomorrow. Stay in touch with us at HackLearning.org, at #HackLearning on Twitter, and on the Hack Learning Facebook group.